Evangelical
Reunion

Evangelical Reunion

*Denominations
and the
One Body of Christ*

John M. Frame

 BAKER BOOK HOUSE
Grand Rapids, Michigan 49516

Copyright 1991 by
Baker Book House Company

Printed in the United States of America

Scripture quotations are from the New International Version.
Copyright © 1973, 1978, 1984 International Bible Society.
Used by permission of Zondervan Bible Publishers.

Library of Congress Cataloging-in-Publication Data

Frame, John M., 1939-
    Evangelical reunion : denominations and the one body of Christ / John M. Frame.
      p. cm.
    Includes bibliographical references and indexes.
    ISBN 0-8010-3560-0
    1. Evangelicalism and Christian union.   I. Title.
BX9.5.E94F73   1991
280 '.042—dc20   91-7182
                                                        CIP

To the churches who nurtured me:

Beverly Heights United Presbyterian Church
Pittsburgh, Pennsylvania

Westerly Road Church
Princeton, New Jersey

Covenant Orthodox Presbyterian Church
Pittsburgh, Pennsylvania

Westminster Orthodox Presbyterian Church
Hamden, Connecticut

New Haven Evangelical Free Church
New Haven, Connecticut

Community Orthodox Presbyterian Church
Blue Bell, Pennsylvania

New Life Presbyterian Church
Escondido, California

Contents

Preface

Although I teach theology, I have never specialized in the doctrine of the church, or "ecclesiology" if you prefer. Still, I have not been able to avoid thinking about the church, the way I have been able to avoid thinking about, say, the timing of the Rapture. In a sense the old saying is true, that if God is our father, the church is our mother. All of what I know about God and about Jesus I have learned, directly or indirectly, from the church. Most of my spiritual encouragement, challenge, comfort, has been through the church. Most of my friendships have been within the church. (I do admire Christians who are able to develop deep friendships with non-Christians, but I don't seem to have that gift.) Most of the love I have known has been in the church. I found my wife in the church, and now my children are growing up in the church. My home away from home is always the church. My favorite music is the music of the church. My favorite people are the people of the church. Many of my favorite times have been times spent in the worship of the church.

I am probably even more "churchy" in my lifestyle than most theology professors. A theologian can justify a certain amount of "church hopping"—spending his Sundays preaching and teaching in one church after another, never putting down roots in a single fellowship. For various reasons of temperament and gifts, I have never felt that God has called me to such an itinerant ministry, although I have no quarrel with my colleagues who do sense such a call. I am a stay-at-home type. I serve on the session of my local Presbyterian church.

Every Sunday I play the piano and lead the congregation in worship. Often I will teach Sunday school as well.

Although my life is probably more church-centered than that of most Christians, I do not consider myself superior to those believers who have not found the sort of fulfillment in the church that I have. Christians, through no fault of their own, find themselves in churches that do not carry out their biblical responsibilities and therefore do not provide the blessings they ought to provide. And some Christians, gifted in evangelism, for example, spend more time than I do out in the world, witnessing to the lost, seeking to bring people into the church from outside. Nothing wrong with that. I do think, though, that the church ought to be important in some ways to all of us, even those in bad church situations or those who are called to labor mostly among the unchurched. It is the *church,* not just individuals, for whom Jesus Christ shed his blood (Acts 20:28, Eph. 5:25–27). And, for that reason, together with the reasons peculiar to my own personality and gifts, I have been unable to avoid meditating on the biblical teachings about the church.

There are other reasons why I keep coming back to this subject. One dates back to 1958, when I was just starting college. In that year, the denomination of my childhood, the United Presbyterian Church of North America, merged with the Presbyterian Church, U.S.A. The UPNA had been relatively conservative in theology, the PCUSA strongly liberal, though with some conservative congregations. Just about that time, the conviction began to dawn on me that "liberalism" was not the Christian gospel.[1] I came to the conclusion that I could not remain in the PCUSA, especially since my PCUSA presbytery at that time was demanding that its ministerial candidates receive training (which I interpreted as "brainwashing") at liberal seminaries. I joined an independent church at that point. But many of my closest friends and respected teachers (notably John H. Gerstner) made other choices, forcing me to rethink and rethink.[2] So my earliest years of theological self-consciousness were focused on denominational and church questions: What is a true church? What obligations are involved in church membership? In what sort of church would God want me to minister?

Another reason for my interest in ecclesiology is that for twenty-two years I was a minister in a tiny denomination (20,000 members, 200 churches) called the Orthodox Presbyterian Church (hence OPC). The editor of a Christian magazine once described the OPC as a kind of continuous theological seminar. Granting some editorial license, I can accept that description, with the footnote that most of the time, as I recall it, the seminar focused on ecclesiology. Like me, the OPC[3] had in 1936 withdrawn from the PCUSA over the issue of theological liberalism. In 1937 the Bible Presbyterians broke away, in turn, from the OPC. Those events were constantly discussed in the OPC; most of us elders heard many opinions about schism, church purity, denominations, and so on. So in those twenty-two years I did a lot of thinking about the church. In 1975 I served as counsel to a fellow minister who was charged with being too sympathetic toward charismatics and others. On three occasions since I was ordained, the church engaged in intensive discussions concerning merger with other bodies. And, during the last of my twenty-two years with the denomination (1988–89), I spent much time pondering, together with my local congregation, whether they and I should stay in the OPC or seek transfer into a somewhat larger denomination (200,000 members, 1,000 churches), the Presbyterian Church in America (PCA). We did make that transfer; the church and I are now PCA. But we did not make the choice without a lot of Scripture searching, heart searching, emotional agony, and intellectual labor.[4]

Through all of that, I have come to certain convictions about the church, particularly about denominations and denominationalism. These are convictions that do not seem to be commonly expressed in the theological literature. Indeed I have not been able to find much agreement to them among the friends with whom I have shared my thoughts. Yet I cannot seem to wriggle away from these ideas, for they seem to me to be the inescapable teaching of Scripture, and I still believe with B. B. Warfield that "what Scripture says, God says." So I have decided to try out my thoughts on the Christian public at large, the trans-denominational body of Christ. If you think I am wrong, please show me how I am wrong; show me from Scripture, please. I am willing, I hope, to change my views in response to a really biblical argument. If you think I am right, see what you can do to change the thinking of others in the church, so that somehow we might, by God's grace, overcome the "curse of denominationalism" that I believe defames our Lord and so often enfeebles our witness.

By "denominationalism," I mean, sometimes (1) the very fact that the Christian church is split into many denominations and sometimes (2) the sinful attitudes and mentalities that lead to such splits and perpetuate them.[5]

I do not look on this book as a scholarly volume, though I trust that it is well informed. It is not a systematic ecclesiology; it will not be part of my dogmatic project, *A Theology of Lordship*. There will not be a lot of scholarly footnotes (though there will be a number of explanatory ones), and I will seek to avoid technical concepts. This book is simply a cry from the heart,[6] but one that I want very much for my brothers and sisters to hear.

I continue to acknowledge debt to many who have stimulated my thinking on this and other subjects. Some are listed in the preface to my *Doctrine of the Knowledge of God*.[7] Here I would like to give special thanks to the twenty-five or so friends who read an earlier version of this book, especially the following, who offered a great many suggestions: Richard Gaffin, James Jordan, Dan Dillard, Thom Notaro, Robert Strimple, Vern Poythress, and Jay Adams (who, very much in character, urged me to add a chapter on "what to do now"). Of course, I take full responsibility for the use of their ideas (and my own!) herein. Thanks also to my pastor, Dick Kaufmann, who shared with me some of his written thoughts about the great need for new churches, which I have interpreted as a ground for thanksgiving that the work of church planting need not be borne only by one denomination (see chapter 4). Thanks also to Presbyterian Heritage Publications who, after I had completed the first draft of this volume, republished a most valuable work from the early nineteenth century, Thomas M'Crie's *The Unity of the Church*.[8] M'Crie was a Scottish Presbyterian minister who viewed at close hand several church splits and attempts at reunion. His scriptural insights have been very helpful to me, and although I differ with him at several important points, I would recommend the book to anyone who wishes to go deeper into the biblical basis of church unity. If someone were to say that the present volume is a kind of updating of M'Crie, I should not argue very much. I wish to acknowledge also the Rev. Arnold Kress who opened my mind to consider some radical alternatives, and three evangelical theologians of our time who have spoken and written cogently about the unity of the church (would that the church had heard them): Edmund P. Clowney, the late John Murray, and Carl F. H. Henry who once wrote in a *Christianity Today* editorial, "Somehow, let's get together."

Notes

1. See J. Gresham Machen, *Christianity and Liberalism*, (Grand Rapids: Eerdmans, 1923), Cornelius Van Til, *Christianity and Barthianism* (Grand Rapids: Baker, 1962).

2. Since I wrote this paragraph, word has come that Dr. Gerstner has joined the Presbyterian Church in America, where I also serve. Welcome, dear servant of Christ!

3. At first it was called the Presbyterian Church of America, a name changed later because of legal problems. This name should not be confused with the present-day body, founded in 1973 and called the Presbyterian Church *in* America.

4. In this book I shall refer from time to time to my experiences in the OPC and the PCA. I grant that these are small bodies and may not be of interest, in themselves, to most readers of this book, who, I hope, will represent many other communions. I beg you, however, not to write off the book as parochial because of these references. I am taking some pains to use examples from other denominations as well; but I must write out of my own experience, and, for better or worse, that experience has been mostly in the OPC and PCA. My editor at Baker Book House urged me to find more examples and illustrations from outside the Presbyterian and Reformed tradition. I tried, but without much success. I am not a specialist in modern church history, and I hesitate to use examples that I have not experienced from the inside, so to speak. And of course besides addressing the broader evangelical constituency, I do also want to say some things to "my own people" that I think they need to hear. If you are neither OPC nor PCA, these references to obscure denominations may help you to gain a more objective perspective on the issues discussed than if I were discussing your own denomination. If you *are* in one of these groups, you may lose the advantage of objectivity but gain the advantage of a more existential or personal involvement. Some readers will need more of the one, some more of the other; I'll trust the Spirit to sort all that out.

5. As I will indicate, not everyone who advocates a split (or the perpetuation of a split) is guilty of sin. Sometimes those who leave a denomination and/or start a new one are in the right; sometimes it is right to turn down an opportunity for reunion. However, it is my firm conviction that wherever occurs a denominational division, and whenever an existing division is prolonged, there is sin *somewhere*. That sin may be in the original group, the seceding group, or both. Most often, in my judgment, the last alternative is the case.

6. Hence the perhaps excessive use of the first person singular pronoun. But that is also because many of my suggestions are tentative and reflect my own rather narrow experience. I do not want to claim too much for these ideas.

7. Phillipsburg, N.J.: Presbyterian and Reformed, 1987.

8. Thomas M'Crie, *The Unity of the Church* (Dallas, Tex.: Presbyterian Heritage Publications, 1989; originally published in Edinburgh, Scotland, by William Blackwood, 1821).

Introduction

This book is not for everybody, though I would not forbid anyone from buying or reading it. In this volume I will be speaking to fellow Christians, those who love Jesus Christ, trust him for their eternal salvation, and are seeking to obey his commands. In my vocabulary and in the teaching of Scripture, the word *Christian* does not refer to someone who merely holds to high moral standards or goes to church or seeks justice in society or admires the teachings of Jesus. Rather, a Christian is someone who has a special relationship, a friendship, with Jesus. For Jesus Christ is no mere historical figure. He is a living person, raised from the dead. Moreover, he is Lord, the supreme Ruler of heaven and earth.

How do you become Jesus' friend? First, by recognizing that no matter how good you may be in your own eyes and in the eyes of other people, you are a sinful person in the eyes of a holy and righteous God (Rom. 3:23). Second, by recognizing that sin against perfect holiness deserves death (Rom. 6:23). Third, by recognizing that you can do nothing to prevent the eternal death that is coming to you, and by throwing yourself upon the mercy of God (Eph. 2:8–9). Fourth, by recognizing that Jesus died in the place of his people (Mark 10:45) and that he offers eternal life to all who trust in that sacrifice (John 3:16). Fifth, by personally trusting Jesus: asking forgiveness on the basis of his shed blood and seeking to obey him as your Lord, your supreme Master.

Further, this book is written to those Christians who have come to see the need to trust and obey God's written word, the Holy Scriptures (2 Tim. 3:16–17; 2 Peter 1:19–21). This book is essentially a Bible study, though it does deal with our present situation as well. My deep conviction is that the Scriptures are God's very voice, speaking to us. Unless you share this conviction, you will think my argument is not very strong. Indeed, it is a weak argument if it is only *my* argument. But, if it is the argument of God himself, we had better pay attention to it and heed it. If the argument is only mine, you can dismiss it politely by saying, "That's very nice, but we would prefer to leave things the way they are." But, if it is God's argument, we had better be willing to make disruptive, dramatic changes. What God says particularly takes precedence over the warm feelings of coziness we have in our present denominational structures.[1]

Before you read the argument, perhaps you should ask yourself whether, *if* God wanted you to help him tear down all the old, familiar denominational structures, you would be willing to join the project. If you are not willing to make such a conditional commitment in advance, you are not one of the ones to whom this book is addressed. Rather, you need to work on the basics of Christian discipleship and godly priorities. I am writing in this book to potential ecclesiastical revolutionaries, to those who are so sold out to Jesus that they are willing to give up many cherished things for him (meditate on Deut. 6:4ff, Matt. 8:18–22, Luke 9:23–26; 14:26; 1 Cor. 9; Phil. 3:1–14). I am writing to those who put the authority of God above the comfort of the status quo.

Denominations, I have discovered, are something of a sacred cow in Christian circles. We often look at them the way a Steeler fan, say, looks at his football team, or the way a patriot looks at his country, or the way a loving son looks at his mother. Our denomination is our team, our country-right-or-wrong, our mother[2] in Christ. We like to see our denomination succeed where others fail, indeed to succeed at the expense of the others. Sometimes we identify such success with the blessing of God. Failure to support the team then turns out to be a kind of blasphemy, almost like renouncing Jesus himself.

To others, the denomination is not so much a team as it is a warm, cozy place to call home. And a man's home, of course, is his castle. When the castle is perceived to be under attack, the attackers must be vanquished. Something very deep inside us calls us to all-out war against anyone who threatens the home.

Perhaps it is foolish for me to write this book, since many will see it as an attack on their team, their country, their mother, their home. Actually, I don't think it is. I think my argument, if implemented, will produce a much stronger team and country, a far more comfortable maternal home. Indeed, rather than destroying all we love and cherish in our denominations, my proposal will preserve all that is good about them far more effectively than we seem able to preserve it today.

Even if the application of these ideas leads to some loss, some sadness, the people of Jesus ought to be willing to make such tiny sacrifices for Jesus. Tiny? Yes, compared with his great sacrifice for us. His sacrifice is the only measure of our love (1 John 4:7–11).

Notes

1. I realize that theological liberals, those professing Christians who do not allow God's word to rule all of life, also are concerned with ecumenism. This book will have little if anything to say about those discussions, about the NCC, WCC, COCU, etc. There are plenty of books and articles on these movements, almost none on evangelical ecumenism (doubtless because there is so little of the latter). Also, liberal arguments for eliminating denominations are not, except in trivial ways, the same as mine, and I wish in this book to address evangelicals very specifically, using distinctively evangelical arguments.

2. The metaphor is certainly not entirely wrong. See the Preface.

Part One

The Road to Denominationalism

1

• •

The One, True Church

We must first be assured that Jesus Christ established on earth one church, not many denominations. Further, the unity of the church is not merely "spiritual," but also "organizational."

The First Churches

The first worshiping community was a family: Adam and Eve expressing their love to God and one another in the Garden of Eden before the fall into sin. Adam, Eve, and God. Satan broke the unity of the family when he tempted Eve to take the forbidden fruit. Paul later wrote: "And Adam was not the one deceived; it was the woman who was deceived and became a sinner" (1 Tim. 2:14). Sin was not a family decision, but a unilateral choice on the part of Eve. She might have consulted her husband, sought consensus. She might have submitted her will to his while he submitted to God. Instead, she separated from her husband; then under her influence he separated from God and made *his* unilateral decision. And when God came to judge (Gen. 3:8ff), Eve blamed the serpent, Adam blamed Eve, and ultimately both of them blamed God.

The fall broke the unity that existed between man, woman, and God. The human family set itself against God and against one another. Indeed, the earth itself was estranged from mankind (Gen. 3:17–19). God showed his great love by promising a redeemer (v. 15). He would draw a re-created humanity back to himself and back to relations of love for one another. But the promise provoked more division, for many people rejected God's love. The first son, Cain, was a murderer, and he became a wanderer on the earth (Gen. 4:8–12). But, in the days of Adam's third son, Seth, and Seth's son Enosh, there was evidently a worshiping community: "At that time men began to call on the name of the LORD" (v. 26).

Scripture tells us little about this early church. But the later pattern of Noah, Abraham, and Moses, together with the contextual preoccupation with genealogies, suggests that the Sethite church was essentially a family congregation, with the patriarch as the chief priest. Therefore it was *one* in an important sense, though unbelief separated it from the rest of humanity.

Even the family of Seth, however, for the most part fell into sinful habits, leading to God's terrible evaluation: "The LORD saw how great man's wickedness on the earth had become, and that every inclination of the thoughts of his heart was only evil all the time" (Gen. 6:5). *But,* we learn: "Noah found favor in the eyes of the LORD" (v. 8). Noah and his family were saved by God's grace from the judgment that destroyed the rest of humanity.

Noah and his family, therefore, were the next "church." The patriarch with his family received God's covenant promise and law (Gen. 8:15–9:17). And Noah was also a prophet, telling by divine inspiration how God would deal with his descendants (Gen. 9:25–27).

The overall pattern, then, is that sin leads to wandering, estrangement, separation from God and from fellow human beings, even from life itself; obedience to God leads to oneness with God and with God's children. God does not approve, however, of every kind of unity. The Cainite cities described in Genesis 4:17–24 represent unity in sin and unbelief, a unity in which evidently (as often in our modern cities) the effects of sin are compounded. The Tower of Babel episode (Gen. 11:1–9) is also a human attempt to recapture unity apart from faith, one that God rejects. But it is interesting to note in Genesis 11 the extraordinary power of unity. God himself testifies in verses 6 and 7: "If as one people speaking the same language they have begun to do this, then nothing they plan to do will be impossible for them. Come, let us go down and confuse their language so they will not understand each other."

Generations later, after the flood, many of Noah's descendants had fallen away from the true God (Josh. 24:2) (though not all—hence Melchizedek [Gen. 14:18ff], Jethro [Exod. 3:1]). But God again gathered a patriarchal family, that of Abraham, Isaac, Jacob. God's covenant separated them[1] from other nations and therefore established them as a unified body. Circumcision marked that unity. Later, under Moses, God gave the people additional signs of unity: three feasts, in which the people were to congregate in a central location—Passover, Pentecost, Tabernacles; one system of sacrifices; one priesthood, proceeding by hereditary succession from Moses' brother Aaron; one order of religious workers and teachers (the tribe of Levi, also united by heredity);. one holy place, the earthly dwelling of God's glory; distinctive garb; distinctive diet; distinctive laws; distinctive promises. In summary, there was one covenant between God and one people: a covenant that distinguished them from all the nations of the earth and therefore united them as one people overagainst all the other nations. Certainly all this reflects the oneness of God himself, which as such sharply separates the worship of Israel from all other nations (Deut. 6:4ff). God's church is to be one, as *he* is one (cf. John 17:11b).[2]

The Central Altar

Much could be said about each of the marks of unity, but let us consider just one of them: the biblical emphasis on a central altar. Deuteronomy 12 teaches that once Israel reaches the Promised Land, God will choose one place "as a dwelling for his Name" (v. 11). All sacrifices are to be offered in that place, not "anywhere you please" (v. 13), as with pagan worship. This emphasis continues through Deuteronomy (14:23ff; 15:20; 16:2–17; 17:8; 10; 18:6; 26:2; 31:11).[3] Political officials, to be sure, are to be dispersed throughout the land, at many locations (Deut. 16:18–20). The Levites, too, are spread throughout the land (Num. 35). But the altar is to be one, at one place.

The central altar did not, however, become a reality for another four or five hundred years. Not until the time of Solomon, the son of King David, did Israel erect a permanent altar in its permanent location, Jerusalem. Finally God had his temple.

Jeroboam, the First Denominationalist

Remarkably, this religious unity in Israel did not last much beyond the reign of the one king, Solomon. Solomon's son, King Rehoboam, was rejected by the ten northern tribes, who founded their own kingdom under Jeroboam. Rehoboam continued to rule in the south over Judah and Benjamin.

The political split was God's doing (1 Kings 11:26–40). But Jeroboam also created a religious split, abandoning the central altar in Jerusalem in favor of two altars in his own territory because he feared that if the people worshiped in Jerusalem, they might again become loyal to the Davidic dynasty (1 Kings 12:25–33). He made the situation even worse by building images of golden calves for the new worship centers (vv. 28ff; cf. Exod. 32). The religious split, as well as the idolatry, displeased God, but Jeroboam made his crime even worse by appointing non-Aaronic priests (1 Kings 13:33f). The name of Jeroboam thereafter became proverbial: he was the one who caused Israel to sin (1 Kings 15:30, 34; 16:2, 7, 19, 26, 31; 21:22; 22:52, etc.).

To God it was truly important, therefore, that his people be religiously unified: one God, one altar, one priesthood. Even political disunity could not justify a religious division. Scripture makes the point over and over and over again: worship at the central altar! Abhor the Jeroboam schism! Were we writing the history of Israel instead of the inspired authors, doubtless we would not have made such a big point of this. But God's priorities are often different from ours, and we would do well to listen to him here.

Exile and Restoration

The unfaithfulness of Israel and Judah led to the loss, in some degree, even of that unity they still possessed as the people of God. That unity could not be lost entirely, as long as Israelite believers continued to call on the one true God. But the prevailing unbelief within these nations led to exile. First the northern and then the southern kingdoms were uprooted and the people were made to live among the pagan-ruled nations of the world.

God determined, however, that this time of exile would end. He prepared the way for reunion by prophecy (e.g., Isa. 11:12ff, Jer. 31:1, 6; 33:6f, Ezek. 36 and 37) and by reformation and revival (Isa. 19:18, 21, 24; Ezek. 11:18f; 36; 37; Zeph. 3:9; Zech. 13:8f; Mal. 3:2–4,), by removing the causes of disunity.[4] Then, of course, he moved the heart of Cyrus to reopen the Promised Land to Jewish rule and immigration (2 Chron. 36:22ff; Ezra 1:1ff; Isa. 44:28; 45:1). God removed the sin of the land (Zech. 3:9), and thus the people returned, no longer divided into two kingdoms. They celebrated the Feast of Tabernacles, the feast of ingathering and reunion (cf. Ezra 3; Neh. 8; Hag. 2; Zech. 14:12–21; Mal. 3:7–12).[5] The dry bones came together by the Spirit of God (Ezek. 37:1–14); Judah and Ephraim again became one (Ezek. 37:19—M'Crie's theme text).

God's Spirit takes away sin and brings revival. Revival removes old divisions and brings God's people together again. That is the scriptural pattern.

The Church in the New Testament

Unlike my dispensationalist brothers and sisters,[6] I believe that the church of the New Testament is essentially the same as the church in the Old, with some changes, of course. It is the "Israel of God" (Gal. 6:16). It bears the same exalted titles given to Israel in the Old Testament (1 Peter 2:9f; cf. Exod. 19:6). The people of God are all one olive tree, a tree from which some branches (unbelieving Jews) have been broken off so that others (believing Gentiles) might be grafted in (Rom. 11:17–32). Promises given to Old Testament Israel are regularly applied to the church in the New Testament. Joel prophesied that God's Spirit would one day be poured out on all people (2:28–32), a prophecy fulfilled by the new presence of the Spirit on the Christians on Pentecost (Acts 2:17–21). Amos prophesied that God would rebuild the tabernacle of David (9:11f), and the Lord fulfills that prophecy by bringing Gentiles into the New Testament church (Acts 15:16–18).

Of course, there are also changes, because major events have taken place: the incarnation, earthly life, death, resurrection, and ascension of Jesus Christ, God's eternal Son. The Aaronic priesthood, the "one priesthood" of the Old Testament, gives way to the new priesthood of Jesus himself, a priesthood disconnected from the Old Covenant in the way that the story of Melchizedek in Genesis 14 is disconnected from its historical context (Heb. 4:14–5:9; and chapters 7–10). The earthly tabernacle and temple, the "central altar," give way to the reality of which they are but shadowy images, the heavenly temple to which Christ brought his once-for-all sacrifice (Heb. 9:11–28). Similarly do the feasts, the sacrifices, the distinctive garb, and the dietary laws give way.

But what of unity? Did Jesus come to establish one church, as in the Old Testament, or many denominations? Does the Old Testament emphasis on church unity fall away with the coming of Christ? If that is the case, it is certainly very difficult to imagine why it should be so. Jesus' one sacrifice obviously eliminates the need for animal sacrifices, a central altar, a continuing human priesthood.[7] But why should it eliminate the need for unity among God's people, that beautiful unity about which the psalmist spoke so eloquently (Ps. 133)?

The need for unity is still there. The New Testament is as concerned about it as is the Old. Please consider the following:

1. *As in the Old Testament, the New Testament believer worships at a central altar.* Christ himself fulfills the central altar of the Old Testament, and there is only *one* Christ (Acts 4:12; 1 Cor. 1:13; 8:6; Eph. 4:4–6). Same for the priesthood, the temple, the sacrifices. The church has a single location in one sense, though it is scattered throughout the earth—for it is seated with Christ in the heavenlies (Eph. 1:3, 20; 2:6; 6:12).[8]

2. *Jesus does come to build one church.* The word *church* is regularly used in the singular to refer to the whole New Testament people of God (Matt. 16:18; cf. Acts 2:47; 5:11; 12:5; 1 Cor. 10:32; 15:9; Gal. 1:13; Eph. 1:22; etc.).

3. *The New Testament church is a unity of a higher order than that of Old Testament Israel.* In the new order, the great schism between Jew and Gentile is broken down. Jesus died not only for the Jewish nation but (as God had spoken—ironically through the wicked priest-prophet Caiaphas) "also for the scattered children of God, to bring them together and make them one" (John 11:51f). At Pentecost, Jews from many nations are united in Christ's body; they participate with *one* "heart and mind" (Acts 4:32). Later, Samaritans (Acts 8) and Gentiles (Acts 10) are added, and the great wall comes down (Eph. 2:11–22; cf. Gal. 2:11–5:26).

4. *There are other ways in which scripture teaches church unity:*

(a)   The New Testament images of the church: a temple, the body of Christ, the bride of Christ, the flock of the Good Shepherd, the branches of the vine, the people (or family) of God—all stress unity in the above senses, but doubtless in many other ways as well.

(b)   There is one Spirit in which we have been baptized, who gives gifts to the church (1 Cor. 12).

(c) It is God's love in Christ that binds us together (John 13:34f;
     1 Cor. 13; 1 John 4:7ff).
(d) There is one gospel (Acts 4:12).
(e) There is one revelation (1 Cor. 2:6–10).
(f) There is one baptism (Eph. 4:5).
(g) There is one Lord's Supper (1 Cor. 10:17).

5. *The New Testament uses the word* **church** *to designate not only the
universal body of Christ* (as above). The word also refers to the
Christians in a region (Acts 15:3), those in a city (e.g., Acts 11:22;
14:23; 18:22; Rom. 16:1), those worshiping together in a household
fellowship (Rom. 16:5; 1 Cor. 16:19; Col. 4:15; Philemon 2)—indicating unity among the Christians at various geographical levels.

6. *The Lord gives his church a church government.* There are first the
apostles and prophets (Matt. 16:18; John 20:21, 23; Eph. 2:19–22;
4:11), but also evangelists, pastors, and teachers (ibid.). Elsewhere
there are references in other terms to church leaders: elders (bishops)
and deacons (1 Tim. 3:1–13; Titus 1:5–9; cf. Acts 11:30; 14:23;
15:2ff, 22f, 20:17; 21:18; 1 Tim. 5:17). Obedience to such leaders is
not an optional matter; it is God's command (1 Cor. 16:16; 1 Thess.
5:12f; Heb. 13:7, 17). We do not, therefore, have the option of
choosing when we will or will not submit to the government of the
church. This is Christ's church, Christ's church government. If we do
not like it, we dare not set up our own government to rival his. Thus,
Christ's intention was to unite all his people under his officers. One
Lord, one church, one church government.

7. *Denominations play no role in New Testament church government.*
Look up *denomination* in a concordance—you won't find it there!
More seriously, whether by *denomination* or by some other name, the
New Testament says nothing at all about what we would today call
denominations. Denominations, in the sense of groups of Christians
who differ from other Christians by some distinctives of doctrine,
practice, ethnicity, or historical background, play *no* role in New
Testament church government.[9] That is especially remarkable when we
consider that there were many diversities in the early church that
might have led its leaders to consider a "friendly" denominational division: great differences of ethnicity, languages, and so on. But the New
Testament seems to make a particular point of stressing that such differences are *not* to be the basis of divisions in the church (Acts 10; 11;
Gal. 2; 3:28; Col. 3:11).

8. *The New Testament rebukes the mentalities and practices that were*

later to produce denominational division in the church. These mentalities and practices are:

(a) *autonomy*—picking and choosing which leaders in the church will have one's respect (1 Cor. 1:10–17; 3:1–23)

(b) *factionalism*—forming partisan groups in the church to advance the program (or supposed program) of one's favorite leaders [same passages as (a)]

(c) *lust for power*—seeking to be boss (Matt. 20:20–28; Acts 8:9–24; 20:30; Phil. 2:1–11; 1 Peter 5:1–3, 3 John 9)

(d) *unwillingness to seek reconciliation*—(Matt. 5:23–26[10]; 18:15–20; Rom. 12:18; Eph. 4:3; Phil. 2:1–4; 4:2; 1 Thess. 5:13; Heb. 12:14; James 3:17)

(e) *failure to maintain church discipline*—(Matt. 18:15–20; 1 Cor. 5)

(f) *inattention to doctrinal and practical purity*—(1 Tim. 4; 6:11–21; 2 Tim. 1:13f; 2:14–4:5; Titus; etc.)

(g) *failure to help fellow believers in need*—(Matt. 25:31–46; 3 John[11])

9. *When Scripture speaks of the church as the body of Christ, it contrasts the harmonious working together of the parts of the body with "schism" or "division."* (See 1 Cor. 12:25, in the context of 1 Cor. 12 and Rom. 12.) The figure of the church as a temple points in the same direction (Eph. 2:21), as does that of the family (Eph. 4:6).

10. *Jesus prayed that the church would be one, as he and his Father are one* (John 17:20f). Now some exegetes understand him here to be referring to "spiritual" unity rather than "organizational" unity. Certainly organizational matters are not the emphasis of this prayer. The emphasis is on the vital union of the believers with Christ in the Spirit. However, that union is not wholly invisible; it is visible in the conduct of Christians in their relationships to one another as well as to God himself. Therefore:

(a) It is doubtful whether ancient readers would have naturally made, in such a context, the spiritual/organizational distinction that we today make so easily.[12]

(b) The unity of which Jesus speaks clearly has a visible dimension, for it is something that even unbelievers can see, and which indeed drives them to faith (v. 21).

(c) The spiritual and the organizational cannot in fact be sharply separated. Our lack of organizational unity is caused by, and in turn causes, the lack of fellowship, harmony, and cooperation that are certainly aspects of, or manifestations of, spiritual unity.

(d) Since it is plain from other texts (above, #3–#6) that Jesus gave a particular government to the church, it is hard to imagine that this (and only this) form of oneness would be excluded from his prayer. Surely he was praying that the church be one in every way that he has established.

(e) Some experts have argued that since Jesus' prayers are always answered, this prayer must be a prayer for spiritual unity (which has, in some sense, always existed in the church) rather than organizational unity (which has not always existed). Do we really want to say that the Father did not answer Jesus' prayer? I have no doubt that the prayer of Jesus will one day be fully answered, that God will unite the church in his own time and will unite it organizationally as well as in all other respects. That seems plain from many other passages. But we also know that God does not always immediately accomplish his will (and that of his Son). For some reason, God often accomplishes his purpose through a historical process that sometimes tries our patience. There is always at least the *beginning* of a fulfillment. Biblical theologians speak of "the already and the not yet." God has *begun* to unify his church (even organizationally!),[13] but there is more unity to come in the future.[14]

11. *Unity is given by divine sovereignty but requires the efforts of human beings.* God's sovereignty in Scripture does not negate, but rather underlies, the efficacy of human efforts. The passages cited earlier make it plain that the establishment of unity is God's work.[15] Yet God himself in Scripture exhorts us solemnly to "keep the unity of the Spirit through the bond of peace" (Eph. 4:3) and to avoid attitudes (above) and actions detrimental to that unity.[16] We are always to seek reconciliation with those whom we have offended or who have offended us (Matt. 5:21–26; 18:15–17). God's sovereignty does not entail human passivity. Scripture's emphasis on God's sovereignty in restoring unity does not undermine human efforts in that direction; rather, it encourages them.

New Testament Church Government

I have already established that God gave to the church a government, that Christians were obligated to honor that government, and that denominations played no role in the government of the church. But perhaps we should go into some more detail about the form of government God gave to the church.

The form of church government is, of course, itself one of the debated matters that has led to denominational division. I shall not try here to resolve the long-running disputes within the church concerning government. I shall, however, summarize the major views on the subject and seek to ascertain the bearing of each on the question of denominationalism.

Congregationalists emphasize the autonomy of the local church body. They do not deny the value of gathering representatives of various churches to help each other in making hard decisions, but they deny the existence of any continuing institution that has perpetual sovereignty over the local church. In their view, all associations of churches are purely voluntary. In one sense, congregationalists are extreme denominationalists, for they regard each congregation as, in effect, a denomination unto itself. On the other hand, if congregationalism is to function well, it is important that each congregation be in fellowship with all the others. When fellowship is broken, one congregation will be unable to associate with another congregation, even voluntarily, to do the Lord's work. Thus, congregationalism is, at another level, anti-denominational. A congregationalism that measures up to the standards implicit in the congregational reading of Scripture would put all the world's churches together in one "congregational association" or "baptist convention."

Episcopal government is even more anti-denominational in its basic thrust. Episcopalianism holds that the churches in each geographical region ought to be ruled (with some checks and balances) by a single bishop. But if this sort of government existed in the early church, the bishop ruled over all the churches in his area, not just those of a particular denomination; and that must still be the ideal for an episcopalian. This anti-denominational thrust will be even stronger for those episcopalians (mostly Roman Catholics and Anglo-Catholics) who believe that the bishops are the successors of the apostles and thus have an additional mandate to rule the churches in their region.

I am a presbyterian. Most likely, I believe, the church was originally organized in a way analogous to the organization of Israel (Exod. 18:17–26), with leaders over tens, hundreds, thousands, and so on. The pattern applied also to Israel's religious life, organized according to families and synagogues, with the Sanhedrin as the highest court. The early Christians naturally adopted this model with little change. The "tens" would be the house churches: essentially single families with, perhaps, others worshiping with them. The "thousands" would be the city churches, the church of Jerusalem, the church of Philippi, and so on—whose leaders Paul addresses as a body in Philippians 1:1.[17]

The highest level would be the whole church; and indeed at one point in Acts a body is convened that has power over the whole church to deal with a matter that could not be resolved at the local level (Acts 15). As such[18] the government of the church is composed of various levels of courts, the broader ones dealing with issues that cannot be resolved by the narrower ones.

This presbyterian structure, like the congregationalist and episcopal alternatives, requires organizational church unity. For if the church is divided into denominations, then (a) there is no highest court by which controversies can be ultimately decided; there are, instead, rival courts; and (b) leaders will be available to help resolve problems only within their own denominations. Denomination 1 will lack the gifts of the leaders in denomination 2, and vice versa. That will be a great disadvantage for both denominations. The resources of each will be less than what God has promised to his people.

Biblical presbyterianism, then, requires the abolition of denominationalism. In a biblically presbyterian church, *all* the area Christians in good standing would vote to elect the elders and deacons. Those officers would rule *all* those Christians, not merely those of one denominational faction. And *all* the gifts God has given his people in the area would be available for the ministry. We can see that biblical presbyterianism is rather different from presbyterianism as it now exists—so different that the latter's biblical warrant is questionable.

My conclusion is that all three of the major views held by Christians regarding church government require for their best implementation the organizational unity of the church and the elimination of denominations.

Notes

1. Note that the gathering of God's people always involves a separation from the world. Separation and unity, then, are correlative in one sense. Not all separations are bad. But it is equally plain that God wants his people to be together. Even "good" separations are a consequence of the fall; had Adam not fallen, there would be no need for a separation between one group called "God's people" and another group called "Satan's people."

2. See Thomas M'Crie, *The Unity of the Church* (Dallas, Tex.: Presbyterian Heritage Publications, 1989; originally published in Edinburgh, Scotland, by William Blackwood, 1821), pp. 9–27. M'Crie notes that since worship is given to one God according to one revelation, it cannot help but be unified.

3. Note the remarkable pervasiveness of this theme. The Lord is emphatic on this point.

4. See the excellent discussion in M'Crie, pp. 70–89.

5. See James B. Jordan, "One in the Spirit," in *Presbyterian Heritage* 10 (Sept. 1986): 1; and his *The Sociology of the Church* (Tyler, Tex.: Geneva Ministries, 1986), p. 101f. Jordan argues that the 70 bulls were sacrificed for the (proverbially) 70 nations of the world, thus suggesting a future ingathering of all the nations.

6. A good recent study of dispensationalism is Vern S. Poythress, *Understanding Dispensationalists* (Grand Rapids: Zondervan, 1988). It is critical, yet sympathetic.

7. Indeed, the movement from many sacrifices to one sacrifice, from many priests to one priest, suggests a historical tendency in the direction of *greater* unity.

8. Note the emphasis in Reformed theology that the church enters heaven in its worship. See Jordan, "One In The Spirit," and his references to Wallace and Calvin.

9. Certainly there is no New Testament basis for using the word *church* to refer to a denomination, as we often do today. Note also that *denomination*, as I use the term, includes independent churches. An independent church, in my understanding, is a denomination all to itself. So we do not escape denominationalism by adopting independency.

10. Note here that seeking reconciliation takes precedence even over the worship of God. That should indicate the high priority that Scripture places on reconciliation. And overcoming denominationalism is a form of reconciliation.

11. Diotrephes appears to be a proto-denominationalist, who refuses hospitality to Christian teachers not allied with his "faction."

12. The sharp contrast between "spiritual" and "material" or "visible" comes from Platonic philosophy rather than Scripture. In Scripture, "spiritual" normally refers to the work of God's Holy Spirit, which can be either visible or invisible.

13. As we shall see, the head of the church organization is the exalted Christ. His is the executive, legislative, and judicial supremacy. In that sense the church is united *organizationally*. Also, God's people are united by the governments of local churches. Denominational governments are unscriptural in my view, but they are better than nothing, and they do unite as well as divide.

14. Those who, like me, stress the organizational unity of the church sometimes receive the exhortation not to neglect the unity that the church already possesses. I believe that in the above discussion I have kept a fair balance between the unity that the church *has* and the forms of unity that the church does not presently have, but which will be given to her in the future.

15. See also M'Crie's excellent observations in *The Unity of the Church*, pp. 57–89.

16. M'Crie also says some valuable things about the human side of it, especially the qualities of heart and life necessary for those who would work for union (*The Unity of the Church*, pp. 118–134).

17. What about the "hundreds"? Well, perhaps there were "local churches" somewhat like those we know today, wherein members of various house churches gathered on occasion. Or perhaps the church simply skipped the hundreds level in the larger cities. It doesn't matter much.

18. The reader may consult more elaborate defenses of presbyterian government if he desires more exposition of these points.

2

$$\ast\ \ast$$

Where Did Denominations Come From?

We have seen that in the New Testament period there was one, true church. Sharply contrasting with that is our situation today, in which the church is divided into many denominations. What has happened—and why?

Even during Bible times there were tendencies toward denominationalism. Remember the sin-inspired separations beginning in the earliest days after the fall of Adam. Remember Jeroboam, the first denominationalist, who "made Israel to sin." We have seen also that the New Testament rebukes attitudes and actions leading to division: unwillingness to submit to authority, autonomy, factionalism, lust for power, rejection of reconciliation, failures of church discipline and of doctrinal and practical purity. The New Testament writers emphasize that there should be no "schism" in the body. Since they issued such rebukes, there were evidently those in the church who deserved and needed them. That is to say, even in the first century, the essential sources of denominationalism were present.

Beyond this, there were also people who left the one, true church.

Some left involuntarily, as the result of proper discipline (1 Cor. 5; 2 Cor. 2:5–11). Others (whom John calls "antichrists") left at their own initiative (1 John 2:18f; 4:3–6). Still others fell away from their initial profession of faith, the texts being inexplicit as to whether these left the church voluntarily or under discipline (Heb. 6:4–6, 10:26–31). Did any of these, perhaps, form sects of their own, claiming to be the true disciples of Christ? We simply don't know; there is no evidence either way.

A Brief History of Denominationalism

In the early centuries following the New Testament period, heresy and schism were more or less synonymous.[1] Heretics, teachers of false doctrine, were church-dividers, schismatics. They sought to attract followers to themselves, either by forming factions in the existing church or by drawing people to leave the church and follow them. The heretic Marcion (approx. A.D. 80–160), who rejected the Old Testament and much of the New, set up many churches dedicated to his philosophy. In the late second century, Montanus, who claimed (but failed to convince the church as a whole) that he brought new revelation from God, attracted many churches to his teaching.

In the mid-third century, however, an event occurred that led to a distinction between heresy and schism. During the Decian persecution, many believers renounced the faith. Afterward, Novatian, a learned priest and theologian, opposed any readmission of these people into the church. The church, however, held that reconciliation could be granted upon repentance. A Roman synod excommunicated Novatian, who then set up his own church, which lasted to the eighth century.[2] The status of the Novatianist church was a matter of some discussion in those days. Those in the Catholic church agreed that schism—departure from the one, true church and establishing a rival church—was a serious sin. Cyprian, Bishop of Carthage, went so far as to deny the validity of Novatianist baptisms, but his principle was not upheld by the church in later years.

Novatian was not considered a heretic, though he did hold a view with which the church did not concur. In general, he was recognized as orthodox in theology, indeed a very competent exponent of Christian truth. He was therefore an "orthodox schismatic." "Heresy" and "schism" were no longer virtually synonymous. Heresy was considered a sin against truth, schism a sin against unity and love.

Persecution, in A.D. 303, gave rise to another schism. As in the earlier case, certain people believed that those who denied the faith under persecution were being treated too leniently by the church. Led by Donatus, these people formed a schismatic denomination that claimed to be, in fact, the one, true church. They rebaptized those who came from the Catholic church. The Donatist church existed until around 700. In the original church, this group, like the Novatianist group, was considered generally orthodox though schismatic.

Another schism developed in the wake of the Council of Chalcedon (451), which declared Christ to be one person in two natures, fully God and fully man. The council's statement was unacceptable to the Egyptian and Syrian churches, and eventually fellowship was broken. That division continues to exist today.

The Eastern Orthodox Churches, under the Patriarch of Constantinople, and the Roman Catholic Church, under the Pope of Rome, broke fellowship in 1054 over the claims of papal authority and the Western insertion into the Nicene Creed the statement maintaining that the Holy Spirit proceeds from both the Father *and the Son* (Latin, *filioque.*) Patriarch and Pope excommunicated one another. That division also continues to the present.

The excommunication of Martin Luther (1521) began a proliferation of divisions: Protestant from Catholic, Protestant from Protestant, sectarian from sectarian. Bucer, Melanchthon Oecolampadius, and Calvin sought unity among the Reformation churches, but without success.

Additional denominations came into existence when the denominations from which they came were thought in some measure to be compromising the true doctrine. Hence the many Reformed denominations of the Netherlands, the many Presbyterian churches of Scotland, the many Baptist denominations of the United States. Still others appeared when people carried their distinctive traditions from one country to another. Often these immigrants wanted to worship with others of the same language and nationality. Thus, in the United States there is an Evangelical Covenant Church (Swedish), an Evangelical Free Church (Norwegian, Danish), a Christian Reformed Church (Dutch), a Russian Orthodox Church, a Korean-American Presbyterian Church, a Church of God in Christ (African-American), a German Reformed Church (the Reformed Church in the United States).

Evaluating the Divisions

How shall we evaluate this complex chain of events? It is not an easy matter. Some evaluations, to be sure, are fairly simple. I do not hesitate to join the ancient church in condemning the schisms of Marcion and

Montanus. These men certainly were heretics, and they had no justification whatever for forming their own "churches." On both counts
they violated scriptural principles. Same for Novatian and Donatus,
though these were relatively much more orthodox than Marcion and
Montanus. The church was right to reject the "rigorist" position of
these men. Novatian and Donatus should have remained in the church,
conforming their views to Scripture and/or accepting the church's discipline for their errors.

The post-Chalcedonian schism, however, is a more difficult issue. I
do believe that the Council of Chalcedon was expressing an important
biblical truth. At the same time, its operative language was philosophical rather than scriptural. In my view, although philosophical language
is not necessarily a wrong means of expressing theological truth, it
tends to raise as many questions as it answers. The council said that
Jesus is "one person in two natures"—but what, precisely, is a "person"? What is a "nature"? How should we interpret the "one person"
so as not to compromise the "two natures," and vice versa? The
answers are not obvious. Lutherans and Calvinists later accused one
another of different sorts of failure to do justice to Chalcedon, and
that debate continues to the present, with intelligent, learned and
godly thinkers on both sides. Is this issue really designed by God to be
a test of orthodoxy?

The Egyptians who rejected Chalcedon (speaking with their Bishop
Cyril of the "one nature of the incarnate word") were called mono-
physites (the root of the word means "one nature"). But the
Egyptians also rejected the extreme monophysite position of Eutyches,
which the council had particularly sought to exclude; so their position
actually agreed with the council in what may be the most significant
respect. Yet they could not accept the formula required by the council.
It is not inconceivable that the Egyptians and Syrians were seeking to
preserve by the "one nature" formula concerns that the majority
expressed by the "one person" formula. If so, the differences between
the two would be merely differences over choice of words.

In retrospect, too, it is evident that there was a lot of sheer power
politics going on in the developments leading to Chalcedon. Personal
loyalties played a considerable role in the theological/terminological
decisions that were made.

The schism was certainly an evil. But who was to blame? Those on
both sides who mixed up theology with partisan loyalty? The
Egyptians, for their unwillingness to accept the verdict of the whole
church, even though their own convictions were perhaps not substan-

tially different? The Council of Chalcedon, for imposing on the people's consciences a difficult philosophical and highly debatable formulation capable of various interpretations and uses? Perhaps there is plenty of blame to go around.

In my Protestant bliss, I can say fairly complacently that the 1054 split between East and West was due to papal arrogance. My Roman Catholic friends are welcome to try to set me straight. But, as for the doctrinal issue, whether the Spirit proceeds only from the Father or from the Son as well, it is hard to imagine why that should be the cause of so momentous a division. It is a very difficult question, one hard to resolve from Scripture. And the concept of "procession" is mysterious indeed, part of the mystery of the Trinity itself. The meaning of it is not at all obvious. I think I can defend the Western position, but I cannot see why it should be made a test of orthodoxy. Certainly one can be a knowledgeable and effective minister of God's word whichever position he takes—or without taking any position at all.

Granting that Luther was right in his doctrinal dispute with Rome, was he also right to start a new denomination? "He was excommunicated," someone will say. "So what else could he do?" Well, he could have continued to teach as an excommunicate Catholic (while rejecting the grounds of the excommunication), praying that God would one day establish his theology in the whole church. Was Luther required to start afresh because the Roman Catholic Church was no longer a true church? But the Reformers did not believe that the Roman Catholic Church had totally lost all the characteristics of a true church. They did not, for example, rebaptize people who had been baptized as Roman Catholics.

The best justifications for starting a new Lutheran church, I think, were these: (1) the Roman Catholic Church was requiring, as a condition of membership in good standing, commission of sin, namely participation in what Luther came to regard as idolatry in the mass; and (2) the church required, as a qualification for teachers, subscription to a view of salvation that Luther believed was flawed at its very core.

Objection: Why should Luther not have remained a Catholic, while recognizing that one with his views could not be "in good standing"? Then, as a "renegade Catholic," he would continue to teach and preach what he believed to be the truth, hoping and praying that in time the church would come to accept his position. The difference between this and starting a new denomination is not great. One might indeed argue that this is in fact what Luther did—he remained Catholic,[3] though not in good standing with the Roman authorities;

he taught, preached, and administered the sacraments to those who
would hear him.

Whose fault was it? Certainly (in my own view, of course) it was the
fault of the Roman Catholic Church for allowing its theology and
practice so to degenerate. Was Luther also to blame for, perhaps,
impatience? Could he not have found a more subtle, gradual way to
bring his ideas to a church for whom justification by faith was shock-
ing and new?

I don't know. Evaluating these matters is very difficult, especially at
more than four centuries' distance. And it is even more difficult to evaluate the various Protestant-from-Protestant splits of the later centuries.
It is clear, however, that all denominational division has been due to sin
somewhere—either among the founders of the new denomination, or
in the previous denomination, or both.[4] The difference between the
church and the denominations is indicated by this fact: that the birth of
a denomination is always attended by sin, but the birth of the church
was attended by rejoicing among the angels of heaven.

Where Is the One, True Church?

The difficulty of evaluating these events means that today it is difficult, if not impossible, to locate the "one, true church" that Jesus
founded in the first century. It would be so nice if we could pick out
one denomination today and say, "This is the one." This would be the
denomination that had never been guilty of unjustified division from
any other body, nor had ever provoked justified division of anyone
from itself. No, there is no such animal. All denominations, so far as I
can tell, are guilty in some measure, at some point in their history, of
schism or of provoking at least a degree of schism.[5]

I am confident in saying that the one, true church until the post-
Chalcedon divisions was the Catholic church, the main body of
Christians. To say that does not necessarily deny the authentic faith of
the members of the Novatianist and Donatist denominations. It does, of
course, say that those people committed sin in leaving the one, true
church. After Chalcedon the picture is not so clear. If the Syrians and
Egyptians were unjustly expelled from the fellowship, they might well
claim that *they* were the one, true church. If, on the other hand, they left
the body without justification, they must be seen as schismatics. But
what if there was fault on both sides? What if the case cannot be neatly
adjudicated? Then it would seem to me that at that point in history

both the Catholics and the dissenters were guilty of sin, and that the one, true church from that time on was to be located in both bodies.

Such ambiguity plagues the history of denominationalism as I see it. Therefore I doubt very much if any denomination today represents uniquely the "one, true church" of the New Testament. The one, true church does, however, still exist! Jesus' promise that "the gates of Hades" will not prevail (Matt. 16:18) has not been broken. But the true church exists today in many denominations, rather than one. It exists in broken form.

The one, true church exists, but its government has been injured. Not entirely, of course. In some ways, the church is still governed the way the church was governed in the first century.

For one thing, we still have local congregations, as they did then. The local congregation is, as it was then, the central bond of Christian fellowship.[6] This represents the "government by tens and hundreds" of Exodus 18. For another thing, the church today still has the same *supreme* court as did the church in the first century. That is the court of heaven where Jesus, the one head of the church, makes the final decisions. At that level, the church is still united and, indeed, at that level has a unified government!

The injuries to the church's government appear, then, at the middle levels, the levels of "thousands" and, we might say, of "ten thousands," "hundred thousands," and "millions." At those levels, the courts of the true church no longer function. In San Diego County, a local church can no longer call for *all* the elders (regardless of denomination) of the region to adjudicate a difficult problem, as I believe the Christians of the first century were able to do. We can call on only the leaders of our own denomination. If I am Southern Baptist, I can call only on the ministers and deacons of the Southern Baptist Convention. If I am Orthodox Presbyterian, I can call only on the elders of the tiny Orthodox Presbyterian Church. So, instead of the courts and fellowships God has ordained, we are left with man-made substitutes, namely denominational courts and fellowships. With those we can get by, perhaps; but there will always be something missing. It simply is not what Christ intended.

How do we restore what Christ intended? That is a difficult question. I don't have any very good answers to it, though I will suggest some preliminary steps in Part Two of this book. Perhaps there are others who can suggest a more complete step-by-step procedure. For now, I want only to insist that we establish unity as our *goal*. Goals are not enough, but they are important. By meditating on them, longing for them, praying for them, we sometimes gain some wisdom on how to achieve them. May that be so in this case.

Chapter 2

1. David F. Wright, "Schism," in *New Dictionary of Theology,* ed. by David F. Wright and Sinclair B. Ferguson (Leicester, England: Inter-Varsity Press, 1988), p. 619.

2. Douglas Kelly, "Novatian," in *ibid.,* p. 472.

3. Surely he did not concur in his excommunication!

4. M'Crie: "When dissensions arise in the Church of God, and it is divided into parties, whatever the occasion or matter of variance may be, there must be guilt somewhere," (*The Unity of the Church,* p. 33). He quotes James 4:1, "Whence come wars and fightings among you? Come they not hence, even of your lusts that war in your members?"

5. Some small Reformed denominations of Dutch origin maintain that, because of scriptural promises, even today there is no more than "one true church," *in every locality.* (I wonder why the "locality" qualification. If scripture promises "one true church" in an organizational sense, then it is implausible to limit that promise to the local level.) They argue that if there are two *apparently* true churches in one locality, one of them at least must be a false church, for one or the other of them is guilty at least of resisting God's call to unity. I applaud the concern for visible unity evident in this argument. Would that more Protestants thought so deeply about it! Yet the argument assumes that a "true" church must be a sinless church, or, perhaps, that sins against church unity are more serious than other sins, so serious as to be incompatible with the status of a true church. Neither of these premises are scriptural. Think of how Paul addresses the wayward Corinthians in 1 Corinthians 1:1ff, and of how the risen Lord addresses the churches of Revelation 1–3. A church can be very sinful indeed, while remaining a true church.

6. To say this is not to embrace congregationalism or independency. Presbyterians and Reformed denominations have always granted a certain "autonomy" to the local congregation. M'Crie: "For the ordinary performance of religious duties and the ordinary management of their own internal affairs, (local congregations) may be said to be complete churches, and furnished with complete powers" (p. 19).

3

❋ ❋

Toward a Post-Denominational View of the Church

It seems to me that far too much of our thinking about the church, both in scholarship and in practical church life, fails to make important distinctions between the church and the denominations. Consider the four attributes given to the church in the Nicene[1] Creed: "one, holy, catholic and apostolic church."

Yes, the church is *one*. As we saw in the previous chapter, even today the one, true church still persists, though with an impaired governmental structure. But the denominations clearly are not one; they are many.

The church is *holy*, not because all Christians and congregations are morally perfect, but because God, in a special relationship, has set his church apart from all other institutions. Scripture gives us no reason to believe that God has placed any human denomination in such a special category, except insofar as it is part of the church as a whole. Among those denominations that are truly parts of the body of Christ, none is in this sense any more holy than the others.

The church is *catholic*, that is, universal. It includes all believers of

41

all times and places. No denomination (even the ones with "Catholic" in their names) can make such a claim.

And the church is *apostolic,* perpetuating the doctrine and life of the apostles of Christ, building on their foundation. As with holiness, a denomination can be "apostolic" if it is faithful to that foundation. But loyalty to the apostles and loyalty to a denomination are not necessarily the same. The apostles, through their writings in Scripture, call us even today to be loyal to the *church* that God built on their foundation. But they do not demand such loyalty to any denomination.

The Gates of Hell and the Free-Will Baptists

Other comparisons may also be illuminating. God has promised that the gates of hell will never prevail against the church—the church will never perish (Matt. 16:18). There is, however, no such promise for denominations. Indeed, many denominations have perished over the years, and often this has been a good thing.

The church was founded by Jesus Christ, out of his unsearchable love. Denominations were founded by human beings, often for at least partly sinful motives.

As we have seen, the church has through its officers a real authority over believers. Has God granted such authority to denominations? I would say that denominations have authority insofar as they do represent the authority of the church (that is difficult to ascertain) and insofar as we voluntarily grant this authority to them in our membership and officers' vows. But this is very different from the authority of the church as such, which is given by Christ himself (Matt. 18:18–20) and is therefore irrevocable.

Scripture promises to the church an ample supply of the Spirit's gifts. To the "one body," God has given sufficient gifts (especially leadership) "to prepare God's people for works of service, so that the body of Christ may be built up until we all reach unity in the faith and in the knowledge of the Son of God and become mature, attaining to the whole measure of the fullness of Christ" (Eph. 4:12–13; note also vv. 14–16 and the teaching of Rom. 12 and 1 Cor. 12). Do modern denominations, *as* denominations, have the right to claim this promise? I very much doubt it. Surely one cannot assume so on the basis of the text's language. And my experience suggests that not all denominations have a balanced and full complement of the gifts of the Spirit. Rather, some denominations have more and better teachers, others more and better evangelists, and so on.

We owe to our fellow Christians a special love ("love for your brothers" [1 Peter 1:22; cf. 1 John 2:10; 3:10ff; 4:20f]), a special care, which takes precedence over our duty to help unbelievers (Gal. 6:10). Is there a special love that we owe only to members of our own denominations and not to other Christians? Although to ask such a question is virtually to answer it negatively, we often act as if it were true. Yes, there are legitimate obligations that we incur to our denominations in our membership vows. But the Christian *philadelphia*, brotherly love, is for the church, not for one denomination above another.

These comparisons should indicate that there are great differences between the church and the denominations: differences in oneness, holiness, universality, apostolicity, power, foundation, authority, gifts, love. Yet it seems that in the ecclesiological literature and in our usual thinking and speaking, we tend to equate the church with the denominations. When Jesus says that the gates of hell shall never prevail against the church, preachers routinely apply that text to the Free-Will Baptist Church or whatever. That is bad exegesis—and bad preaching.

We need an ecclesiology that makes some careful distinctions between the attributes, powers, and gifts of the church, on the one hand, and those of particular denominations, on the other. We should no longer develop doctrines of the church that are written as if the schisms had never taken place, or as if we were all still living before 451.

If someone seeks to stir up in us passions of denominational loyalty, we must raise questions by pointing to Scripture's very high view of the church. The church is a wonderful thing, deserving our deepest loyalty. Jesus shed his own blood for the church. Denominations are another thing altogether. I am not saying that we owe no loyalty to our denominations, but that such loyalty must be tempered by the understanding that these organizations are the result of sin and are inadequate human substitutes for the God-given order of the one, true church. Somewhere in each of our hearts ought to be the conviction that denominations should work to their own extinction, not to their own glorification.

A Practical Case

It is fairly obvious that Novatian and Donatus should not have left the one, true church to start their own churches. They were, in truth, "schismatic." Sometimes today, one believer will call others "schismatic" when they leave one denomination to join another. Is that fair?

I do believe that it is possible to commit the sin of schism today. Most of the time, when people start *new* denominations and thus *add* to the divisions in the body of Christ, I do not hesitate to call them schismatic. Similarly will I do so when they leave one denomination for another for the same motives Novatian and Donatus had: pride, unwillingness to submit to legitimate discipline, desire for autonomy.[2] But in many (perhaps most) situations where people make such transfers, there is no schismatic behavior at all. The true church is scattered among many denominations today. Transfer is often simply a matter of wanting to go from one part of the church to another, to share the gifts of Christians in a different group. Let us become clear on this: Leaving the church is one thing; leaving a denomination quite another. The former is a serious matter, the latter much less so.

This is the sort of practical case that makes it dangerous for us to identify the New Testament church with some modern denomination. That confusion can lead to unfair judgments against one another. Instead we should seek to make the right distinctions, to judge wisely. The church is found in the denominations; but the denominations are not the church.

In my view it is misleading for denominations to take names for themselves with "church" in the singular: Protestant Episcopal Church, Presbyterian Church in the U.S.A., Presbyterian Church in America, and so on. "Church" in Scripture is never used for anything like a denomination. Better to speak of "churches," indicating an association of local congregations (as in the Dutch "Reformed Churches in the Netherlands"), for it is biblically correct to use "church" to refer to a local congregation.

We are in a post-denominational age, and we must apply the Scriptures to the times in which we are living, not to a time that is long past. It is not easy to find the precise continuities and discontinuities between the church and the denominations. But we must be willing to take up that task.

Notes

1. Actually, Niceno-Constantinopolitan, from the Council of Constantinople of 381.
2. Schism also occurs when people unnecessarily resist church union and those practices that lead to further union.

What's Really So Bad
About Denominationalism?

In the preceding chapters, I have given a number of reasons why the church should not have been divided into denominations. *First,* Christ founded one church and commanded us to preserve its unity. Denominations have no role to play in biblical church government; rather they are destructive of that government. *Second,* the denominational division of the church has always been the result of sin—on the part of the founders of the new denomination, or on the part of their original denomination, or both. The people involved should have solved their problem by biblical reconciliation, not by denominational division. *Third,* denominationalism has imposed on us the burden of subjecting ourselves and our congregations to human organizations that cannot claim in full the promises and the gifts of God.[1]

Those should certainly be sufficient reasons for us to seek the abolition of denominationalism. Clearly, denominations are contrary to God's will. Those who are servants of God need to know nothing more.

But some will complain, "Wait a minute. Denominations aren't really so bad *in practice*. Whatever else can be said, we can live with them. We

45

are able to worship, preach, teach, evangelize, plant churches, share the sacraments, carry out discipline, and support Christian social action in the present denominational structure. Indeed, denominations have often been helpful to the ministry of local congregations, giving them financial assistance, encouragement, fellowship, leadership, mobilizing believers to pray, helping to resolve difficulties. If the system ain't broke, why fix it?"

This kind of talk is, I think, usually a symptom of ignorance or spiritual immaturity or both. It attempts to reject scriptural principles on the basis of essentially pragmatic considerations. Yet it does have some legitimate force. One might agree that denominations are a problem "in principle" (which many mistranslate "in theory"), but feel at the same time that since denominationalism is not doing much *practical* damage, the problem may be placed on the back burner. Though God has mandated us to reunite the church, someone might say, we may rightly give that project a lower priority than others that are more immediately pressing.

As I shall indicate later, I do believe that we must make priority judgments even among divine commands, though we certainly may not "prioritize" any of God's commands out of existence, as some might prefer in this case. However, I must reject the premise that denominationalism is not doing any "practical" damage. Indeed it is doing a great deal of damage, and the fact that this damage is invisible to so many people makes it all the worse.

Disobeying God always leads to practical damage. Obeying God brings blessing, disobeying him brings curse (Ps. 1). One of my working titles for this book was *The Curse of Denominationalism*. I rejected it as too much of a negative, "downer" type of title, though it certainly had the appropriate kind of shock value. The issue is serious and the church is asleep to it; we need rousing language at times such as these. But even more we need to see the curse up close, the concrete damage that denominationalism does in our midst. In the next chapter I will discuss the supposed benefits of denominations alluded to in the third paragraph of this chapter. Here I want to list some very practical *disadvantages* of denominationalism:

1. *Denominationalism has greatly weakened church discipline.* Discipline is one of the traditional "marks of the true church" that I shall discuss in a later chapter. A church without discipline is a church without means of maintaining a united gospel testimony. Scripture requires discipline, which includes teaching, exhorting, rebuking, but which in extreme cases can lead to excommunication (Matt.

18:15–20; 1 Cor. 5; 2 Thess. 3:6–15; 2 Tim. 4:1–5). In the first century, when someone was disciplined by the church (granting the exhaustion of all possible appeals) that discipline was respected by all believers. Today that is no longer the case. Sadly, in most of our churches today there is no formal discipline. Yet even those churches that seek to implement biblical discipline are frequently frustrated by denominationalism. Suppose that Bill is excommunicated from First Baptist as an unrepentant adulterer. Often, Bill will then be perfectly free to go down the street and attend, say, First Methodist, as a member in good standing.

Part of the problem is that there are no consistent standards of doctrine or morality among our denominations. First Methodist may simply be a more liberal church than First Baptist. Another part of the problem is that denominationalism hinders communication among churches. First Baptist may conscientiously inform the other local Baptist churches of its action, but since they cannot write to all the churches of other denominations, First Methodist does not receive the message. And Bill is not going to tell them.[2] A third part of the problem is that denominationalism fosters among churches an ungodly competitiveness, rather than cooperativeness: First Methodist may be so happy to get someone away from the Baptists that they don't even trouble to ask the former church about Bill.

Since discipline can be a rather unpleasant business to begin with, and since its purposes are so easily frustrated (as in the above example), many churches abandon it altogether, except for preaching and teaching. Yet, without discipline, the whole moral and doctrinal condition of the church of Christ deteriorates. Certainly our denominational divisions must take a good part of the blame for this sad situation.

2. *Because of the denominationalism-inspired decline in discipline, church membership means very little today.*[3] People take membership vows to be subject to their brothers and sisters in the Lord, but those vows often mean very little. Members often attend for a few weeks, then disappear without speaking to anyone. They will join other churches without ever bringing their grievances before the church they have left (*contra* Matt. 18:15ff). They can get away with this because denominational division has both provided them with many places to go and has broken down communication between churches. Rather than resolve their grievances in a biblical way, they simply disappear into another denomination, and there is no machinery for finding them and calling them back to their responsibilities. Such people do not perceive the church as having any *authority* over them, or themselves as having

any "one-anothering" *responsibility* to the body. They have no desire to bear the burdens of the body to which they have sworn loyalty.

Denominations demand the loyalty of believers to themselves, but, ironically, they undermine the loyalty that is far more important, the loyalty of believers to their local congregations.

3. *Because of denominationalism, there is in the church an imbalance of spiritual gifts.* As I indicated earlier, God promises to give his church an adequate and full supply of the gifts of the spirit: leadership, serving, teaching, encouraging, giving, showing mercy, and so on (Rom. 12:1–8; cf. 1 Cor. 12; Eph. 4). He has not, however, made such a promise to denominations. Membership in the church is determined by God's Spirit, as the Lord adds people to his church (Acts 2:47; 13:48). God is also sovereign over the membership of denominations; but he does not guarantee to each denomination an ideal mix of people and gifts. Denominations tend to be populated essentially by people who have similar interests and backgrounds. Especially today, denominational membership is based less on doctrinal commitment than on ethnic, socioeconomic, and social factors. Therefore, certain denominations have a disproportionate number of intellectuals; others the salesman types whom God often uses as effective evangelists; others the big-hearted, generous folk who like to focus on the needs of the poor; still others artistically talented folk who make good organists and choir members.

And denominational barriers often frustrate the communication of these gifts from one denomination to another. A church of one denomination may face formidable barriers when it seeks to benefit from the ministry of someone in another denomination, even when the two denominations are very similar in doctrine and practice. Thus, denominations frustrate the expressed purpose of God to provide *all* believers with *all* gifts of the Spirit by giving all believers to one another.

4. *Because of denominationalism, the church lacks common courts to resolve disputes.* If Calvary Baptist believes that Trinity Episcopal has been using unbiblical tactics to steal its members, who can resolve that dispute? It is possible that the Baptist church may appeal to the Episcopal bishop and obtain some redress. What if, after all appeals are exhausted, the highest courts of the Baptists and the Episcopalians still disagree? Then the matter must be left unsettled, for there is no common court that has jurisdiction over both churches.[4, 5] Indeed, in most cases, we don't even try to resolve disputes like that, contrary to Scripture's teaching (Matt. 5:23–26; 18:15–20; etc.).

This obstacle has also prevented resolving the outstanding historical disputes among denominations over doctrine and practice. Shall we baptize infants or not?—or shall each congregation (or each individual) be permitted to do as it (or he/she) pleases? If that question had arisen in the first century, there would have been courts of the church competent to make a decision for the whole church. Today such courts do not exist. So Episcopalians decide one way, Baptists another way.

5. *Denominationalism hardens existing divisions.* In this world, sin will persist, even among believers, until the return of Christ (1 John 1:8). Thus, there will always be among believers some strifes, disagreements, and estrangements. Since in our denominational age there are no common courts to resolve such differences, trans-denominational estrangements can only fester and become worse. Is it not possible that twenty centuries of Spirit-led study of Scripture in a united church might by now have led to some universally plausible consensus on such disputes as infant vs. believers' baptism or the nature of human freedom? However, the denominations today lack the fullness of the Spirit's gifts, they lack the wisdom of Bible students in other traditions, and they lack common courts. So, rather than making progress on these matters, Christians tend instead simply to defend positions taken in the past and to hurl new epithets at their opponents in the other denominations, epithets that must be replied to, and so on it goes. Rather than the church drawing together around the Word of God, its component denominations move further and further apart.

6. *Denominational division makes reconciliation more difficult*—reconciliation, that is, of the estrangements that led to the division. As M'Crie says, "It is easy to divide, but not so easy to unite. A child may break or take to pieces an instrument which it will baffle the most skillful to put together and repair."[6] Among separated brethren, insults and recriminations multiply; stories of injuries are retold with more attention to rhetorical force than to accuracy. New decisions are made in each group without consultation with the other, and these often become new sources of controversy, which now cannot really be resolved because of the denominational separation. Since these new controversies reinforce the separation, denominations often remain apart long after the original reason for their separation has disappeared.

7. *Denominationalism creates unholy alliances.* We should not ignore the fact that just as there is a biblical doctrine of church unity, there is also a biblical doctrine of *separation:* separation from evil. Thus, ministers often vow to seek not only the "peace and unity" but also the "purity" of the church. Many of our denominations, however, are anything but pure. Their theology is contaminated by liberalism

and often discipline is too weak to cope with outright immorality. Therefore, Christian believers often find themselves allied ("unequally yoked," as Paul says [2 Cor. 6:14]) to those who have repudiated God's Word. Their money and efforts go into promoting teaching and lifestyles that in many cases are the exact opposite of biblical Christianity. It is often said that there are greater divisions *within* denominations today than there are *between* denominations. A Bible-believing American Baptist has much more in common with a Bible-believing United Methodist than either has with liberals in his own denomination. So why don't the evangelical Baptists and evangelical Methodists get together and support one another? Why shouldn't they promote one another's mission efforts and literature rather than in effect promoting missions and literature that they radically disagree with? The answer seems to be denominational loyalty. When denominational loyalty reaches this point, does not God call us to repudiate it? Is it not at this point that Paul's admonition, "Therefore come out from them and be separate" (2 Cor. 6:17) has application to professing Christian denominations? However we look at this issue, we must certainly not try to find the solution in a renewed denominational pride. That pride is precisely where the problem lies.

8. *Denominationalism compromises the church's witness to the world.* Jesus prayed, "May they be brought to complete unity to let the world know that you sent me and have loved them even as you have loved me" (John 17:23b). One important reason why Jesus wants his church to be one is that it will thereby be a more effective witness to the unbelieving world. Disunity obviously raises questions about the divine origin of the church. People naturally ask, "If the gospel is a divine revelation, why are there so many disagreements as to what it means? If Jesus is the Son of God, the Lord of love, why don't his people love one another more? Why all the backbiting, insulting, contending?" Unbelievers have often used the church's divisions to excuse their unbelief. I don't, of course, accept the validity of that excuse; but I very much regret the necessity of having to explain why the church is "God's people" even though it is so miserably divided.

9. *Denominationalism leads to creedal stagnation.* The ancient church formulated creeds in response to various problems that arose.[7] The period following the Reformation led to a great many Protestant creeds, and, indeed, to Roman Catholic responses such as the decrees of the Council of Trent. The Roman Catholic Church has continued to publish authoritative documents from time to time, decrees of councils, papal encyclicals on various subjects, episcopal letters. The

Eastern Orthodox churches recognize no councils or creeds beyond those of the classic seven ecumenical councils held prior to A.D. 800. Protestant denominations have occasionally published creeds or doctrinal statements even in modern times, but that has been rare, and those documents have not attracted much support outside their original denominations.

Surely there have been major issues before the church in all the ages of its existence. And surely there are many issues in the general society that the church ought to address. The fact that the church has not done so is largely because it can no longer speak with a single voice. A creed written by Roman Catholics would have little support among Presbyterians, and so on. Indeed, in the current situation, new creeds may be counterproductive to the best interests of the church. The ancient creeds tended to foster unity, drawing the church together to speak with one voice. Today, however, creeds seem more often to attract the criticism of Christians in other bodies and to stand in the way of unity. I would oppose any new creed for my own denomination, because any such creed would be a barrier to merger with any other denomination. It would be one more thing requiring "discussion" and "negotiation."

Thus, in various ways, denominational division discourages creed writing. That in turn blunts the witness of the church to the world and prevents the establishment of clear standards within the church on current issues. And, since most of the existing creeds are from earlier ages, the church's attention tends to be focused on the past rather than on issues urgently calling for attention today.

10. *Denominationalism leads to distorted priorities,* causing Christians to be preoccupied with the affairs of their denomination rather than with the broader concerns of the church. Much energy is devoted to studying the denomination's history, defending its positions, financing its activities, trying to attract believers from other bodies into one's own denomination, and showing how bad the other denominations have been. In other words, Christians spend much time and energy on matters that in God's sight are either detrimental to the work of the kingdom or are at best matters of low priority. "Majoring in the minors," they develop ingrown outlooks,[8] focusing on preserving and defending a denomination rather than bringing unbelievers into the church. Often this process leads to negativist mentalities, in which more energy is put into criticism of other Christians than into the positive proclamation of the gospel.

11. *Denominationalism leads to superficiality.* Most Christians today

take spiritual nourishment only from their particular denominational traditions. Some of these traditions are richer than others, but none is as rich as the tradition encompassing the entire worldwide church throughout history. Many are hungering for something more meaningful than what they have experienced. Some Presbyterians are seeking depth in the traditional liturgies of the Catholic and Orthodox communions. Some charismatics are seeking a more profound understanding of the Bible and are meeting that need by reading Reformed theology. But all of this is happening in spite of the denominational structure, not because of it. Because people usually have to go against the grain of their fellowships to accomplish this, the present denominational structure of the church is an impediment to those who would seek greater depth in their Christian lives.

The superficiality exists in many dimensions. I spoke above about worship and theology. Being a theologian, I am particularly struck by the lightweight character of much theology today, as compared with that written in the times, say, of the Puritans, the Reformers, or even of the medieval and post-Reformation scholastics. Surely much of this is due to the growing domination of denominational traditions over theological thought. Here, as in the general life of the church (above, #8), there is a "majoring in the minors" and a tendency to labor with past historical issues rather than those confronting the church today. I also note a tendency toward intellectual dishonesty, as theologians engage in special pleading for their own denominational traditions while forcing themselves in spite of actual evidence to find evil in other traditions. Some have overcome this theological narrowness and have become "ecumenical" theologians, but these are mostly theological liberals who distort the gospel in even more serious ways than the ways noted above.

I am not asking Reformed theologians, for example (such as myself!), to surrender their belief that the Reformed faith is the most consistently scriptural system of doctrine yet devised. I am only suggesting that it is not necessarily a perfect system, and we may be able to learn from our brothers and sisters in other traditions. Is it really likely that the Holy Spirit has given such wisdom to one branch of the church so that it will be right about *everything*? Though I love the Reformed faith, and though I believe it to be true on the basis of my current level of knowledge, I do not know all the other forms of Christian theology well enough to say that the Reformed tradition has attained the absolute final truth on every matter. Indeed, I expect to find some theological surprises when I get to heaven. Can we not all seek to be a bit more teachable?

Denominationalism works against us. Most theologians teach in seminaries. Because those seminaries are expected to prepare students to defend denominational traditions, an "us against them" mentality develops. It is not easy for a theologian in such an atmosphere to admit to some defects in his own tradition and to some advantages in someone else's. That leads to superficial theology.

12. *Denominational-related superficiality is naturally connected with parochialism.* Most denominations are limited to a single country, though the church of the first century was quite explicitly and intentionally transnational. Therefore, most Christians are preoccupied with matters close to home at the expense of a proper focus on the whole world as God's harvest field. Recently the "world Christian" movement has developed, seeking to instill in believers a greater awareness of the needs of countries other than our own. That is all to the good, in my view, though I think the world-Christians sometimes neglect the diversity of gifts in the body, talking as if all were called to be thoroughly preoccupied with far-off lands. Again the problem is made worse by denominationalism. Early Christians were very much aware of the needs of their brothers and sisters in other lands; they were constantly being reminded of it by the apostles, who themselves were leading the missionary movement. It is hard to imagine how any merely national body could stir up equivalent passion for missions.[9]

13. *Parochialism leads to a weakening in the worldwide solidarity of Christians.* There are not only unbelievers in other lands who need to hear the gospel; there are also fellow believers who often need our prayers and support. Of course, we do often pray for those foreign churches where our denominational missionaries labor. But we often forget those of other denominations and traditions. Consider the Roman Catholics of Poland, who showed great heroism in the face of terrible opposition by the Communist system. How much did we for them in their time of need? Or do we Protestants consider Roman Catholics too far beyond the pale? How about the churches in the Soviet Union, largely Russian Orthodox, Baptist, and Pentecostal? Have those of, say, the Presbyterian tradition adequately upheld these brothers and sisters? Can any of us Christians claim to match the support that American Jews have given to Soviet Jewish dissidents? Many unbelievers would naturally conclude from the facts that Jews love one another far more than do Christians. Do we want that judgment to stand as the last word?[10]

14. *Denominationalism provokes unhealthy competition among denominational groups.* Typically, we seek to enlarge our own denomination and decrease others by our efforts at church planting and church growth. Often we find ourselves in direct competition: an Orthodox Presbyterian Church competing with a Christian Reformed Church to see who can get the greatest number of local Calvinists; or a Baptist church and an Independent Bible Church competing for the local dispensational population.

A more scriptural outlook, however, is that we desire to plant churches and see church growth, *not* so we can get a larger share of the population for our own denomination at the expense of another, but so that we may reach more non-Christians for Jesus. In view of our Lord's Great Commission, our concern should not be merely with the portion of the community that belongs to our tradition, but with the community at large, Christian and non-Christian. With that outlook, we can see that there really need be no competition at all. No denomination can possibly do the whole job. When we see the dimensions of the evangelistic task before us, we will be thankful that there are denominations besides our own to help out (more of this in chapter 7).

15. *Denominationalism leads to ungodly pride and snobbery.* We tend to take pride in the accomplishments of our own denomination. That is not entirely bad, as we shall see in the next chapter. It becomes bad if that pride leads us to disregard what God is doing in other parts of the church and therefore to look down on Christians from other traditions. Indeed, it is often the case that people from outside a certain denominational tradition are made to feel unwelcome in churches of that denomination. I once visited a church that worshiped according to a much more formal liturgy than did my own. The people all knew when to stand, sit, respond, kneel, and so on. I did not know these things, and no one bothered to inform me. Neither were they published in the bulletin or anywhere else that I could ascertain. I felt very much left out of it all, and I did not discern among the people around me any particular sympathy for my plight. They had their tradition, and it was their church. They knew what they were doing, and if any visitor did not understand, that was too bad for him.

Indeed, sometimes the snobbery is even worse. Since many denominations are based on a common ethnic heritage, visitors who come from a different background often feel left in the cold. Pity the African-American who wanders into a Dutch-American church, or the WASP who invades a Swedish-American fellowship. The emphasis on ethnic ties in our nation's churches often borders (at least) on racism.

Even if a church is not racist, it is often in danger of welcoming only those of a particular socioeconomic level or those with certain levels of education. Possibly because some church-growth theorists tell us that relatively homogeneous bodies are the most likely to grow, many churches today are *intentionally* geared to reaching only one group of people, classified by ethnicity, economics, education, and so on. I am not such a social revolutionary as to insist that these homogeneous units be broken down. Indeed, it is natural that people with common situations and interests make friends with each other, and I don't see anything wrong with that. But no one should ever be turned away from a church because of his or her economic or social status (James 2:1–7). No visitor should ever on that account be unwelcome or unloved.

The homogeneous character of a church is usually a function of its denominational attachment. Presbyterians tend to be wealthier than Baptists, for example. Even if there were no denominations, individual congregations would no doubt still be relatively homogeneous. But each upper-middle-class church would be in solidarity with, say, a church a few blocks away that ministers mainly to the poor. And the poor would have a voice in our church courts. The poor would then be less easily ignored by the wealthier churches—and vice versa. And there would be less room for the complaint of the liberation theologians that the theology of the West is too much the work of one socioeconomic group.

There may be other problems of denominationalism that I have not mentioned. But, after this survey, can anyone seriously say that denominationalism does not cause *practical* problems for the church? Can anyone deny that there would be considerable benefits in abolishing denominations?

Notes

1. Students of my Doctrine of the Knowledge of God will note that these reasons are first normative, then existential, then situational. That fact occurred to me only after I had written first the first three chapters and then written the above summary of them.

2. That scenario may seem implausible, but it has happened often in my experience. Perhaps, in a more plausible example, Bill would move to the next town, where he is relatively unknown.

3. The situation has become so bad that the very idea of church membership requires defense among some people. Briefly, the defense is this: God calls us to obey our leaders (Heb. 13:17) and to bear one another's burdens (Gal. 6:2). These obligations mean nothing if they are not undertaken toward a particular body of believers with their leaders. To undertake such obligations is to take a membership vow. Also, the leaders need to know specifically whom they are responsible to serve (Matt. 20:20–26; Acts 20:28–31); it is not too much for us to allow them to put our names on a list. Such a list, however, is a membership list.

4. Except, as we mentioned earlier, for the highest court, the court over which the Lord Jesus presides in heaven. But the verdict of that court may come in too late to restore cooperation among the churches in our time.

5. Presbyterians should recall my comment in chapter 1 that the lack of common courts at local, regional, and national (even international) levels shows that a truly biblical presbyterianism has not been practiced in modern times.

6. Thomas M'Crie, The Unity of the Church (Dallas, Tex.: Presbyterian Heritage Publications, 1989), p. 41f.

7. If anyone requires a justification for creeds and an account of the best way to use them, see my Doctrine of the Knowledge of God (Phillipsburg, N.J.: Presbyterian and Reformed, 1987), pp. 225f, 305ff.

8. For a good discussion of this, see C. John Miller, Outgrowing the Ingrown Church (Grand Rapids: Ministry Resources Library, Zondervan, 1986).

9. Miller (ibid.) also focuses well on this problem area.

10. After I wrote the above material, God did some wonderful things in Eastern Europe and the Soviet Union for which I (and I trust all of us) am deeply thankful. I only wish that my prayers had been more of a factor in bringing about these changes.

5

❋ ❋

Denominations:
Why We Love Them

O ne might sympathize somewhat with my argument against denominations up to this point yet feel very uneasy about it. The uneasiness is, I think, connected with the fact that my argument has not dealt with the *positive* side of denominationalism. After all, most Christians[1] see denominations as good guys, not bad guys, in our warfare for the kingdom of God. As I indicated earlier, denominations give individual Christians and congregations many benefits, such as financial assistance, encouragement, fellowship, leadership, mobilizing believers to pray, helping to resolve difficulties.

Some have argued beyond this a view known as "pluriformity" or "complementarity"—that denominations are a God-ordained means of accommodating the diversities among believers. In other words, people who like fast, rhythmic music can join denominations that use such music in worship; people who hate such music can join denominations that exclude it. Or Christians who believe in infant baptism can affiliate with a Presbyterian church; those who cannot accept that doctrine can join the Baptists. That way, according to the theory, each denomination is spared from constant internal bickering, and everybody is free to follow his conscience or indulge his preferences. It's a bit like a zoo where high fences keep the natural enemies apart and maintain peace for all. Indeed, the fences enable us, on occasion, to speak civilly to Christians of other denominations, even to work with them in some limited ways, without worrying that their heretical ideas will infect our own congregations. Denominationalism therefore allows for amicable, civilized "divorces" among believers.

However, God did not establish a zoo, but a church. His plan for dealing with estrangements is not amicable divorce, but mutual discipline *within* the church (Matt. 18:15–20; 1 Cor. 5). (This can, to be sure, sometimes lead to excommunication when a really serious problem cannot otherwise be overcome.) We are to be accountable to one another. The natural result of that accountability is unity of mind (Eph. 4:1–16; Phil. 4:2) or, in some instances, agreeing to disagree in love, within the fellowship of the one, true church (Acts 15:37–40; Rom. 14; 1 Cor. 8).

Kinds of Diversities

It is important for us to distinguish between the different kinds of diversities if we are to evaluate properly the claim of denominationalism to provide the best ordering of diversity. There are:

1. *Diversities tolerable within the one, true church.* Certainly God intended the one, true church to include much diversity, for we are diverse people—in culture, personalities, spiritual gifts. Had the church remained united, there is no reason why there could not be wide differences among congregations as to the kind of music used, the style of preaching, the types of ministries provided, and so on. There is room for differences on many such matters within the fellowship of believers. We certainly do not need denominations to provide opportunities to express such diversity.

2. *Intolerable diversities.* On some other matters, there is *no* room for diversity. If someone is preaching "another gospel," he is under a curse (Gal. 1:6–9). Since such preaching must be excluded from the church, it certainly would not be sufficient for the heretic to transfer by amicable "divorce" into his own denomination. The church's relationship to those who deny the heart of the gospel should not be amicable. From such we are simply to turn away (2 Tim. 3:5), not to honor them as interdenominational colleagues.

3. *Difficult cases.* Sometimes, however, the tolerability of a difference is itself a matter of controversy. Take the difference between those who

do and those who do not baptize infants. Some might argue that this difference is tolerable: that people on both sides of the question recognize people on the other side as fellow believers, holding forth the true gospel. Others argue that the difference is substantial: that since baptism is, among other things, the public entrance of persons into the visible church, differences over the subjects of baptism are necessarily differences over the membership of the church. There is therefore disagreement as to who is a Christian and who is not. Is it tolerable to have a church that is uncertain as to its own membership?

Personally, I think uncertainty in this area *is* tolerable, and I will say more about that in a later chapter. But what I think is rather unimportant. The important question is: How does God want us to resolve such differences? And the only answer can be: through the courts of the one, true church. Only such courts are fully qualified to judge which side is right and to determine the limits within which the church may tolerate error. Therefore, the existence of such problems does not in itself necessitate denominational division. Rather, such problems make church unity all the more important. It is hard to imagine how the church will ever resolve such questions until some measure of unity is restored.

Denominational Services

But what of all the good things denominations do for us—the financial assistance, encouragement, fellowship, and so on? Well, is it not obvious that all these things could be done, and in many cases done better, by a *united* church? Imagine the resources we would have! If a poor family faces a $500,000 medical bill with no insurance, very few denominations, much less congregations, would be able to afford to give more than token diaconal assistance. But what if we could appeal to *all the Christians in the world* for help? We could more than handle it. Indeed, why should not the church diaconate set up its own health-insurance program for all Christians and only Christians? The costs, I should think, would be less than commercial insurance, since it would be nonprofit and many major risk factors (smoking, alcohol, and drug abuse, etc.) would be relatively low. And everyone would be taken care of. Denominations cannot afford to think big in that way; but God's united church can.[2]

This approach would work similarly for the other alleged benefits of denominational membership. Imagine the new dimensions of Christian fellowship we would experience by befriending fellow believers from all national and socioeconomic backgrounds and being exposed to a wider variety of personalities and interests than we have known in our denominational fellowships. Imagine the prayer support that could be raised up for the matters that are important to God.

My Home, My Family, My Team

If you are still not persuaded, I think I know why. Most likely it is the feeling of uneasiness we all have with any radical proposal. One can call it fear of the unknown—or be more sympathetic and call it a deep love for the familiar.

A denomination is a kind of home, a place where we can feel comfortable, where we will not be bothered with pressure to make radical changes. It is also like a family, a group to whom we will always be free to give our love and to expect the same in return. And it is also like a home team, which sometimes wins and sometimes loses, but with which we stick through thick or thin. Homes, families, and teams are never perfect. But when they are *ours,* they are enormously precious.

Such relationships are easier to form with people who are like ourselves in interests, abilities, socioeconomic status, ethnic background, and so on. As mentioned earlier, most denominations are fairly homogeneous in those respects. It is hard for most people to think of leaving such a homogeneous structure, going into some unknown alternative that may not be as pleasantly familiar. But I do think that our legitimate need for homogeneity can be met by relatively homogeneous congregations within an *overall* nonhomogeneous church. Such a congregation can certainly play the role of home and family, while offering opportunities for wider fellowship among our universal "extended family."

Can it also play the role of home team? Perhaps that is the rub. So much of our denominational life is structured according to "us" against "them." It's West vs. East, Protestant vs. Catholic, Presbyterian vs. Episcopal, dispensationalist vs. covenant theologist, charismatic vs. noncharismatic, anabaptist vs. paedobaptist, even "our kind of baptist" vs. "their kind of baptist." Some of this is a legitimate attempt to distinguish what one believes to be true doctrine from its counterfeits. But it can mislead believers into thinking that their main warfare is with other Christians. On the contrary, the great gulf is not between anabaptists and paedobaptists or between Presbyterians and Episcopalians, but between belief and unbelief, between Christ and the evil one.

I do honestly hope that the presbyterian form of government will eventually prevail in the church over the episcopal and congregational forms. Some of you may hope that won't happen. But such concerns, both yours and mine, must be secondary to the prayer of our heart, "Even so, come, Lord Jesus," a prayer for the soon coming of God's righteous kingdom, which will rid the world of all evil. In my judgment, denominationalism tends to influence us to reverse this priority.

A Christian's home team, family, and spiritual home should be nothing less than the one, true church. That church is the only institution among human beings guaranteed to prevail over its adversaries. Though we cannot be sure that any denomination will prevail over the others, we can be sure that Jesus' church will triumph. We should get used to rooting more for "the church" and less for a particular denomination.

Toward a Balanced Denominational Loyalty

Does all this mean there is no place for denominational loyalty? Must we discontinue all support of our denominations and instead work for their demolition? I think not. Rather, we should support them *and* work for their demolition at the same time!

Denominations are not the church, but the church is in them and they are in the church. While certainly not God's first choice as a means of governing his church, they are better than nothing. And denominational officers, whether called pastors, elders, bishops, or deacons, deserve our allegiance because they are also officers of the one, true church, whom God has raised up. We should continue to pray for them and support them with our gifts and talents. Denominational missionaries are missionaries of the church, and they, too, deserve our support, in most cases.

Furthermore, of course, many of us have taken vows to be subject to the denominational bodies of which we are members. A vow is a very serious commitment between ourselves and God. We have no right to break those vows, except when keeping them would force us to disobey God.

Another point is that many of us belong to a particular denomination because we conscientiously believe in some or all of its distinctive teachings and practices. If conscience so constrains us, it will also constrain us to pray and work for the triumph of those distinctives in the church at large. As a conscientious Presbyterian, it is only consistent for me to pray, work, and hope for the triumph of Presbyterianism. And I realize that conscientious Episcopalians and Congregationalists must also, at the risk of inconsistency, pray, work, and hope for the triumph of their convictions. That is one legitimate form of denominational loyalty.

Even denominational pride is not entirely wrong, but it needs to be brought into focus. When I was a minister of the Orthodox Presbyterian Church (OPC), I was very proud of what God had done through that body. Though it was a tiny denomination, it boasted the leadership of a remarkable number of the leading scholars in the evangelical church, men like J. Gresham Machen, Cornelius Van Til, Edward J. Young, Meredith G. Kline, John Murray, R. B. Kuiper, Edmund P. Clowney, Harvie M. Conn, Jay Adams. I was pleased that evangelicals of many other denominations looked to these men for theological leadership. I still am pleased at that fact, though I now belong to another denomination, the Presbyterian Church in America (PCA). The PCA is remarkable, I believe, because it recently boasted the fastest-growing missionary force of any denomination. It, too, has included a remarkable proportion of ministers recognized as leaders throughout the evangelical world: D. James Kennedy, R. C. Sproul, James Montgomery Boice, the late Francis Schaeffer, Arthur Glasser, Edmund P. Clowney (yes, he moved, too), George Grant[3] and many others.[4] I will boast of the PCA, and I will also boast of the OPC! And of the Reformed Baptists (Al Martin and Walter Chantry are among the best preachers ever), the Missouri Synod Lutherans (who courageously purged their denomination of theological liberalism), and all the rest. It is right to rejoice in God's gifts to particular denominations, because these are also God's gifts to the one, true church.

I boast of the OPC's steadfast adherence to its doctrinal standards, but not because it happened in the OPC. I boast of that because it happened in the one, true church—in this time and place, by the grace of God, the one, true church was steadfast. The reference to grace, of course, is important: ". . . no more boasting about men!" (1 Cor. 3:21); "Let him who boasts boast in the Lord" (1 Cor. 1:31b; 2 Cor. 10:17.)

Again, denominational loyalty is not entirely a bad thing. It just needs to be brought into balance. Presbyterians ought to be good Christians first and good Presbyterians second, without neglecting either loyalty. They should be good Presbyterians because their Presbyterian denominations are part of the one, true church. But they should be good Presbyterians *second,* because a Christian's first loyalty is always to God and to the one, true church that he founded. Similarly, though Methodists ought to be faithful to their Methodist churches, they should be seeking ways and opportunities to eliminate the separate existence of Methodism.

We ought to love our denominations while seeking to destroy them. A paradox? No, not really. Perhaps *destroy* is not the best word.

On the day when, God willing, all the denominations are re-absorbed into the one, true church, nothing of value need be destroyed. All that is good and blessed about our denominations should continue and be raised to a higher level. Ungodly pride, false doctrine, and division, should be destroyed, not those qualities that really make our denominations lovable.

Indeed, for many (perhaps all of us), denominational loyalty *requires* us to seek the reunion of the church of Christ. The Roman Catholic Church, as its name implies, places a very high premium on catholicity, the universality of the church; and it now reaches out to its "separated brethren." Anglican Episcopalianism also aspires to catholicity, to welcoming Christians of many emphases and traditions. Calvin was one of the strongest ecumenists among the Reformers (following his predecessors Zwingli and Oecolampadius, as was the Lutheran Melanchthon. Modern Calvinists and Lutherans must continue to work for unity if they are to be true to their own heritage. John Wesley worked with Christians of many different backgrounds and had no intention of starting a new Methodist denomination.

Congregationalists and Independents have historically been strong critics of denominationalism. And Pentecostals often rejoice at how the gifts of the Spirit draw together Christians of different backgrounds. It is when the denominations are most true to their traditions, that they are most ecumenical. But when they allow themselves to be distracted by pride and denominational chauvinism, when they are ruled by the instinct for self-preservation rather than the self-sacrificial spirit of Jesus, they erect barriers to reunion. We need to be *better* Episcopalians, *better* Presbyterians, *better* Lutherans, Methodists, Baptists, Congregationalists, Pentecostals, Independents, and whatever else there be.

Notes

1. Except the independents, who in my vocabulary are, despite their antidenominational rhetoric, really one-congregation denominationalists.

2. The Church of Jesus Christ of Latter-Day Saints, often called "Mormon," is a cult whose teachings are deeply unbiblical. Yet, through tithing and a unified worldwide organization, they are able to take care of their poor and needy in a way that should put most Christian churches to shame.

3. And now, as of July, 1990, John H. Gerstner!

4. It is interesting to note that the "famous names" of the OPC are primarily theologians, while those of the PCA are primarily pastors and popular teachers. That says something about the difference in character, indeed the difference in spiritual gifts, between the two groups.

• •

Some Roads Back to Unity

6

❋ ❋

God's Plan for Reunion

In Part One, I have tried to show how denominationalism emerged out of the one, true church of the New Testament and how that development is contrary to God's will. Now I shall try to sketch some ways by which the situation might be remedied, some steps that may in time work to restore the unity of God's church.

My title for Part One, "*The Road* to Denominationalism," is more confident than my title for Part Two, "*Some Roads* Back to Unity" (italics added!). The first part is historical, and I believe it is fairly clear from history how we have gotten into our present predicament. However, the way back to unity is not nearly as clear to me. I think it is obvious that God wants his church to be united and that he will bring about its unity in his own time. But what of human responsibility? What can *we* do? Here I can only suggest some possibilities, some thoughts that *may* be of help. But I cannot say I know whether, when, or how God may choose to restore unity in his church.

Like Part One, Part Two represents a very individual point of view, one doubtless in need of correction from others in the body. I have had few precedents to guide me along this road. Hence the perhaps excessive use (for a theological work) of the first-person-singular pronoun.[1]

One important step is for us to recognize what sorts of things continue to keep us apart and to develop a proper biblical understanding of those barriers to union. That biblical perspective may give us the insight and motivation to judge others more fairly. We may then be more willing to recognize weaknesses in our own traditions and to set aside, at least tentatively, the assumptions about other traditions derived from our historical polemics. Alternatively, while continuing to affirm the superiority of our own traditions, we will discover more effective ways of persuading others of our convictions. Unity will be enhanced in either of those ways.

In the next chapters, I shall discuss some of the major causes of continuing divisions and some ways in which we may be able to draw closer to one another. This chapter, however, will focus on the one fact that is certain: that God himself intends to unify his church and that therefore the reunion of the church is his work. M'Crie says:

> A happy reunion of the divided Church is promised in the Word of God. It is implied in those promises which secure to the Church the enjoyment of a high degree of prosperity in the latter days—in which God engages to arise and have mercy on Zion, to be favorable to his people, pardon their iniquity and hear their prayers, cause their reproach to cease, and make them a praise, a glory, and a rejoicing in all the earth; in a word, in which he promises to pour out his Holy Spirit and revive his work. God cannot be duly glorified, religion cannot triumph in the world, the Church cannot be prosperous and happy, until her internal dissensions are abated, and her children come to act in greater unison and concert. But when her God vouchsafes to make the light of his countenance to shine upon her, and sheds down the enlightening, reviving, restorative and sanctifying influences of his Spirit, the long delayed, long wished-for, day will not be far distant. It will have already dawned.[2]

It will be noted that M'Crie is a postmillennialist. For those who reject this point of view, his argument can be reconstructed to point to a time *after* Christ's return when the unity of the church is restored. However:

1. Even amills and premills must leave open the *possibility* that God might perform this work before the end of this age; surely they cannot prove that God *will not* do this.
2. Even if God's sovereign reuniting of the church will not be completed until the return of Christ, partial unions of various kinds are still possible.

3. The normal scriptural pattern is what scholars call the "already and not-yet"; that is, the blessings promised in the New Heavens and New Earth are already present in seed form. Salvation, for instance, is both future and present (and past) in the New Testament. Therefore, even if complete unity is delayed until the return of Christ, we ought to be able to see the beginnings of that unity in the church today.

4. Scripture presents the New Heavens and New Earth as a guide for our decisions here and now. If we truly look forward to the righteousness of the last days, we should be seeking it now (Matt. 6:33; 2 Peter 3:13f; 1 John 3:2–3).

So, if we really look forward to the reunification of God's people, we should be seeking it here and now.

This complication, however, should not obscure the force of M'Crie's overall point: that God intends to remove the effects of sin from his church and therefore also to remove disunity which, as we have already seen, is always the result of sin.

M'Crie also mentions a number of specific texts in which God promises the reunion of his people. Many of these are in the Old Testament (Ps. 60:1f; 85:3ff, 10f; Isa. 11:12ff; 52:8; 56:8; Jer. 31:1, 6, 10; 33:6f; Ezek. 37:19–22; Zeph. 3:9). One may refer these to God's gathering Israel out of exile and reuniting them in the Promised Land. Still, it is important to remember that this ingathering is a picture of what God intends to do through Christ in gathering people from *all* nations into his church. In the Old Testament itself, there are prophecies of unity that cannot easily be assimilated to the post-exilic return of Israel to Palestine. In Zechariah 8:20–22, we learn that "many peoples and powerful nations will come to Jerusalem to seek the Lord Almighty and to entreat him" (v. 22). Compare with this the passage in Isaiah 19:16–25 concerning the future conversion of Egypt and Assyria, at which time: "The Egyptians and Assyrians will worship together. In that day Israel will be the third, along with Egypt and Assyria, a blessing on the earth" (vv. 23–24). That vision of an internationally unified church certainly anticipates the New Testament period, the time long after the Jewish exile.

That God intends to reunite the *New Testament* church is also evident in those texts that speak of reunion under the messianic Son of David (Ezek. 37:22, 24; Mic. 4:3; Zech. 9:10). Jesus is the "Prince of Peace" (Isa. 9:6; cf. Ps. 72:7), who makes peace by "his blood, shed on the cross" (Col. 1:20). It is he who prays for the unity of his church (John 17:21).[3] The church's contentions and divisions await the word of the Son (Isa. 32:13ff) so that "the Spirit is poured upon us from on high" (v. 15a). And indeed we learn from the New Testament that it is the Spirit who creates in us those qualities of character most conducive to unity (Eph. 4:3; cf. John 16:13; Rom. 1:4; Gal. 5:22–26).

"God prepares the way for union," M'Crie continues, "by reformation, and the revival of real religion."[4] This is the difference between true and false peace (Jer. 6:14; 8:11; cf. 2 Kings 9:19–22). God's reunion will come about, not by compromise of the truth or indifference to God, but by a revival of devotion to Christ and his truth. Note the connections between reformation and unity in Isaiah 19:18, 21, 24; Jeremiah 3:14–17; Ezekiel 11:18f; 20:37–40; 36:23–27; Zephaniah 3:9. Note the same connections in the story of Hezekiah (2 Kings 18:4; 2 Chron. 30:11–26), and in the return from exile (Ezra and Nehemiah).

The reader will profit from following M'Crie further: "God sometimes facilitates and prepares the way for union by removing the occasions of offense and division,"[5] he argues, and then later, "God prepares the way for union in his Church by causing the divided parties to participate in the same afflictions and deliverances."[6] M'Crie's biblical observations in these areas are most edifying.

At least one thing is evident from our brief survey of biblical materials: *The unity of the church is a major theme of Scripture, and God intends to accomplish this union.* Refer also to my discussion in chapter 1, which seeks to show that organizational disunity is contrary to God's will. Surely, because God intends to remove all other forms of sin from his people, this form of sin will also be eradicated.

We can be thankful then, that God's sovereign power stands behind the movement toward church unity, weak as that movement may appear from a human viewpoint. God will surely bring it to pass, in his time.

What of *our* time? Since God's eternal intentions are secret to us, I do not know how much unity God intends to give to the church in this age, any more than I know what degree of moral maturity God intends to bestow on the church in the next ten years. Yet, in both cases, I believe God blesses efforts to achieve, when those efforts are rooted in his grace. He honors those who seek his goals, even when, for his mysterious reasons, he withholds from them success in their own time (cf. Deut. 29:29). Just as Protestants honor Wycliffe and Huss, though their movements were unsuccessful by human standards, I believe that God honors those who work for church unity, even when their efforts bear no apparent fruit.

As I argued earlier, God's sovereignty is not opposed to human responsibility. Rather, the former undergirds the latter. We are encouraged to seek God's kingdom because we know that God is bringing his kingdom to the earth. We also know that God's sovereign plan regularly makes use of human agents to accomplish divine goals. So it is evident that God wishes us to do what we can to rid the church of its divisions. In the coming chapters I shall be making suggestions as to what human beings can do. But let us never forget that the work is "not by might, nor by power, but by [God's] Spirit" (Zech. 4:6).

Notes

1. But see my *Doctrine of the Knowledge of God* (Phillipsburg, N.J.: Presbyterian and Reformed, 1987), pp. 319–322, where I argue that theology must always be a personal response to God's grace.

2. Thomas M'Crie, *The Unity of the Church* (Dallas, Tex.: Presbyterian Heritage Publications, 1989), pp. 57–58.

3. As I indicated earlier, God *has* answered Jesus' prayer by creating the unity that already exists in the church. But there is more unity yet to come—another example of the "already and not yet." God always accomplishes his will; but for some mysterious reason he doesn't always accomplish it *immediately*. Often he accomplishes it over a slow (to us) historical process. Similarly, God always answers the prayers of his Son; but he doesn't always do that immediately either. In some ways, aspects, degrees, God has yet to *fully* answer the prayer of his Son.

4. M'Crie, *The Unity of the Church*, p. 70.

5. Ibid., p. 78.

6. Ibid., p. 82.

7

⊛ ⊛

Denominations
in Perspective

Maturity involves learning to see things in proper "proportion" or "perspective." Little children tend to get very upset over things that in later life will not disturb them. The reason seems to be that as we grow older, we tend to take larger and larger contexts into account. Even as adults, we still spill orange juice; but compared to the great questions of human existence, we feel that the spill is not worth fussing about. We still may wonder, as children do, why we have to comb our hair each day; but that is no problem compared to others we experience in adult life.

It is important that we also learn to see our denominational traditions in broader contexts, from different angles, in different settings. It is easy enough to be denominational chauvinists if we never encounter anyone from any other tradition. It is not so easy when we meet real flesh-and-blood fellow Christians from other branches of the church. This is especially the case when God calls us to stand together with them against unbelief. In this chapter, let us imagine ourselves in various situations that might lead us to question some of our normal assumptions.

A Neighborhood Bible Study

My wife once regularly attended a neighborhood Bible study with women from Roman Catholic, charismatic, Arminian, dispensational, and Episcopalian backgrounds as well as some fellow Presbyterians. However, it never became a doctrinal battleground, she says, because the study always focused on the text of Scripture. The women sought to avoid technical theological jargon and tried simply to do justice to what the Bible taught.

Certainly they studied some passages that were heavy with doctrinal content. Romans 9 was one. When the group read Romans 9, Calvinist and Arminian together marveled at God's control of history, including the human heart. When they got to Romans 10, all with one accord were challenged with the responsibility of human beings to preach the gospel. No one insisted on the dogmatic terminology of "free will" on the one hand, or of "unconditional election" on the other. Romans 9 and 10 spoke for themselves, as it were, and bound these Christian women together in praise and fellowship. All sincerely and warmly received the scriptural message.

Perhaps someone will say that they missed something! A Calvinist might reply that unless we bring in the theological concept of unconditional election, we cannot possibly understand Romans 9, and that therefore the ladies in question were rejoicing in ignorance. An Arminian might say the same thing about "free will." But if God did not inspire Paul to write the words *unconditional election,* why should we insist that those precise words—or the words *free will*—are necessary to express his meaning?

I have no doubt that the women understood Romans 9 and 10. Would the theological terms have helped them get a *better* understanding? Perhaps in some Bible studies, but not in this one. In this particular case, introduction of technicalities would have produced unnecessary quarreling—certainly not the response the apostle Paul (and God, the ultimate Author) intended the text to evoke. And the use of such terms might have exaggerated the extent to which Paul himself had a technical theological purpose in writing these chapters. No doubt an avoidance of technicalities in this particular context gave the women a *better* understanding of the passages than they would have had otherwise.

Paul wrote these chapters at a time when the Calvinist/Arminian, even the Augustinian/Pelagian, debates were still future. He was not trying to persuade Arminians to become Calvinists, or the other way around. It is not wrong for us today to use these passages to help resolve the controversy. But it *is* wrong to suggest that this is their only legitimate use or even their chief use, or that the texts can be understood only in the context of that debate. Rather, there are other contexts too—other uses, such as the ones Paul actually had in mind.

Certainly divine sovereignty and human responsibility are major themes of these passages. But one may appreciate both themes without concentrating on the historical controversies over them. The ladies in the Bible study praised God's sovereignty, and they accepted the scriptural challenge to their own responsibility. And they did it without argument and without debate, simply listening to the Word of God. For them, for an hour or so, the church was one.

Are there not times even in our local church life when it might be best simply to let the text speak (more or less! for we are still "explaining" it to one another) for itself? Do we always have to point out, in expounding Romans 9 and 10, how our party is right and the other party wrong? Does not that very emphasis keep us from appreciating certain nuances and emphases in the passage? Does not that practice exaggerate the importance of the historical controversy?

My wife (like me, a good Calvinist) says that it is not hard to convince people of Calvinistic teachings when you avoid using Calvinistic jargon. I agree. Beyond this, there is a slogan among the Reformed that "anyone who prays for another's conversion is a Calvinist." I'm not sure where that came from; it has been attributed to Warfield, Van Til, Vos. I agree with that, too. If you pray for the soul of another, you believe that person's decision is in the hand of God, not merely a product of the person's "free agency." But many pray like Calvinists, while proclaiming Arminian theology. That seems inconsistent to me, but I welcome their prayers and will be happy to have them pray with me for the conversion of sinners. So perhaps my wife's point can be taken a further step, for there are people around who are Calvinists in one degree or another (evidenced by their words and actions),[1] who would not use the Calvinistic jargon, who perhaps would even repudiate it.

It seems to me that what we call Calvinism is simply a spelling out of the heart instincts of all believers in Christ. I can easily persuade myself that the whole church will be Calvinist eventually, if we allow people to read Scripture as it stands, without feeling that we have to rub their noses in historic controversy. There is a certain "smarty pants" theological attitude in wanting to show people of the other party that our team was right all along. We sometimes feel that we need to do that to make our case maximally cogent; but in fact that attitude *detracts* from the cogency of our case. We give people the impression that to acknowledge the biblical principle they must also acknowledge us, our denomination, our historical traditions. But no. Although biblical principle deserves their allegiance, our "team" does not necessarily deserve it.

The last two paragraphs, to be sure, are written from the viewpoint of a convinced Calvinist. An Arminian, however, might have written some similar statements from his point of view—for example, that everyone is an Arminian when he urges someone to make a decision for Christ. I disagree. But the larger point is clear; people express their theology in various ways: verbal, nonverbal, technical, nontechnical, consistently, inconsistently. We should not assume that the only way, or the best way, to teach Scripture is from a technical theological perspective. Sometimes people can agree on a nontechnical level while disagreeing on the technical level. I cannot believe that this nontechnical agreement is necessarily confused or insignificant.

My point here is not that we can simply convert our denominations into the sort of "neighborhood Bible study" described above and thus abandon all our distinctives. My only point is that it is possible and often desirable to teach the Word of God *without* a stress on denominational distinctives, history, and so on. I am not saying we must always teach it that way. I am saying that if we experienced more of the blessings my wife experienced in her Bible study, we would have a better sense of the reality of the universal church and the relativity of denominational traditions.

The sort of unity my wife experienced in her neighborhood Bible study I have also experienced, especially in pro-life activity. In a recent rally I attended, the most eloquent speaker by far was a Roman Catholic priest, and he was at his best when he spoke of salvation through Christ alone. Oh, yes, he also mentioned that he addressed Mary in prayer. He carefully explained that he did not worship Mary, but that she was part of the communion of saints and he desired her fellowship, as he desired that of living saints, in bringing his requests to God. I still do not share his assurance that Mary hears our prayers and in some fashion relays them to God; but somehow in that context the distance between my views and those of the priest—on that matter, anyway—did not seem terribly far apart. He was fighting—far more heroically than I, for he had been to jail often for his convictions—a battle for Jesus and for the little ones made in God's image. I have no doubt that he and I are fighting the same battle.

Before we talk about dissolving denominations into church unions, we need an influx of new vision. We need to be able to see the church/denomination relationship from various perspectives. I think that when we do this we will be able to distinguish better between church and denomination, between divine institution and temporary human expedient.

A Military Chaplaincy

Here's another "perspective." A fellow minister in my presbytery is a navy chaplain. He is a pretty strict Calvinist, zealous to maintain doctrinal purity in the church. He would, I have no doubt, strongly oppose any candidate for the Presbyterian ministry who was charismatic in his theology.

Yet, in a recent report of his work as a chaplain, he told the presbytery that God had given him a fellow worker who was a member of the Assemblies of God. The chaplain rejoiced, for this worker was a real evangelical believer who preached the gospel. There was little if any conflict between them; the theological difference seemed small compared with the great gap between the Christian and the non-Christian servicemen.

I could not help but remark (mentally!) that my fellow Presbyterian was rejoicing in a kind of alliance that he would certainly repudiate within his denomination. Nor would I, to be honest, want to allow free rein to charismatic theology within our Presbyterian denomination. But it impresses me that the work of God can in some situations be advanced despite differences such as these. It seems that when God's workers are in situations where they are relatively free from denominational constraints and where they are in the front lines of the battle against Satan's wickedness, denominational differences, even theological ones, become less significant, and the unity of believers against the forces of evil becomes more so.

I am not prepared now to ask us to abandon all our denominational connections and to do all our evangelism through such *ad hoc* alliances. I do think, however, that the more we look outside our denominations to focus on the great needs of the unconverted, the more common ground we will find with Christians of other traditions. Some of us have learned to distinguish between inward- and outward-facing churches.[2] The former type of church is concerned largely with its own maintenance, its own integrity, its continuity with historical tradition, the nurture of its own members. The outward-facing church focuses on the world outside the church; thus it concentrates much more effort on evangelism and missions. The two differ largely in emphasis; inward-facing churches usually do give *some* attention to missions, and outward-facing churches are concerned with theological integrity and Christian nurture. But often the differences in emphasis are substantial. Outward-facing churches are not against the nurture of their members;[3] but they are convinced that Christians grow best when they are active in carrying out the Lord's Great Commission in Matthew 28:19–20. I suspect that if all of our churches were more "outward facing" (as military chaplains must be almost in the nature of the case), we would have a more positive view of Christians from other traditions.

A Foreign-Missions Viewpoint

Regularly I have observed that when foreign missionaries return home for furlough, they tend to have grown in their appreciation for Christians outside their denomination. The foreign missionary is often lonely for Christian fellowship, especially fellowship with Christians from his or her home country. Denominational connection is relatively unimportant. And, as with military chaplains, foreign missionaries are of necessity "outward facing." They see unbelief and its cultural fruits up close. To them, the great chasm is not between Baptist and non-Baptist, or Episcopalian and non-Episcopalian, but between believer and unbeliever. They lose, to some extent, their denominational chauvinism.

Consider yourself in such an environment. Would you not be pleased to find another Christian missionary to work with, even one with a somewhat different (but not radically different) interpretation of Scripture?

This development is not toward doctrinal indifference. I have seen very few (if any) missionaries return with a lessened conviction of the importance of the Christian gospel. Indeed, most have had their Calvinist (or Baptist or Arminian or whatever) convictions reinforced to some extent. The development is rather toward a renewed appreciation of one's doctrinal tradition, *along with* a greater respect for Christians outside that tradition and an ability to work together with them.

This situation exists not only in foreign countries, but anywhere that the church is small, immature, and/or threatened by powerful adversaries. It exists in the inner cities of the United States, in minority communities. It exists in corporations where a few Christians get together to pray and to seek ways of applying biblical standards on the job. It exists on university campuses where Christians of different denominational backgrounds seek to stand together against the fashionable secular humanisms of our time. My guess is that the Christians who are the most excited and zealous about their faith are those who have at some time been on the front lines in such environments. In such situations we swim or we sink; we either become more dependent on God or our spiritual life goes into regression. In such situations we get a clearer insight into the universal spiritual battle. We see that serving God requires effort (by grace) and dedication. And we also see that Christians must "hang together or hang separately." On the front lines, denominational differences almost always seem less important. It is no longer Baptist versus Presbyterian, but Christian versus unbelief.

Is it not possible that we have lost perspective in our relatively comfortable home churches? Might we not look at our denominations differently if we had to engage daily in the struggle for the hearts and minds of unbelievers? Might a more outward-facing mentality lead to a more genuinely ecumenical spirit?

A Home-Missions Perspective

Let us face that last question more directly. I have some friends in a small midwestern community who worship in a Presbyterian church that some years ago faced some unexpected competition. A Presbyterian denomination different from that of my friends decided to plant a new church within the same community. There was much weeping and wailing in the first church, for they feared the new church would come in and take away some of their members. The planters of the new church had not contacted or consulted the members of the older church. In my opinion that was wrong, but I am now inclined to think that much of my friends' weeping and wailing was out of place. I can certainly sympathize with their reaction, for I used to think the same way. I can remember actually being happy once when a nearby church closed its doors, for I hoped that several of its families might start coming to *my* church.

But, of course, in the deepest sense it was not my church, it was God's. And God builds his church with far more wisdom than humans do. He has, I believe, led me to change my thinking about church rivalry.

Win Arn reports, "In 1900 there were 27 churches for every 10,000 Americans. In 1985 there were only 12 churches for every 10,000 Americans. There are approximately 340,000 churches in

America. Based on the best estimate and research, we could *double the number of churches* without overchurching America."[4]

My pastor, Dick Kaufmann, has graciously furnished me with the following additional statistics. There are approximately 420 evangelical churches in San Diego County. These have altogether a seating capacity of 126,000, so if each has two Sunday morning services, they could accommodate 252,000. However, there are at least 1,848,000 unchurched people living in San Diego County. The number of them that could be accommodated in the existing church buildings is minimal. Clearly, if we are to expect God to convert substantial numbers of non-Christians, we would have to greatly increase the sizes or the numbers of churches, or both. Increasing the numbers of churches (that is, planting new ones) seems to be the most successful strategy for reaching the unchurched.

Let us consider, then, what is necessary, humanly speaking, to reach San Diego County for Christ. To have 10 churches for each 10,000 unchurched (slightly less than the 1985 average and far less than the 1900 average), we would need to have 1,848 new churches *now*. To have the same ratio in the year 2000, we would have to have 2,448 new churches.

Even the relatively small city of Escondido (present population, 97,000; expected to rise to 147,000 by 2000) will need many more churches if the unchurched in the city are to be reached. Kaufmann estimates that Escondido needs 83 new churches to reach the 10 per 10,000 ratio today. (Its present ratio is 4.5 churches per 10,000.) To do the same in 2000 will require 133 new churches. To maintain even the present ratio of churches to population in the year 2000, God's people would have to plant 60 churches.[5]

Statistically speaking, we are losing the battle. Arn[6] says that in the United States Protestantism is shrinking from two-thirds of the population in 1900 to one-third (estimated) by 2000. Between 80 percent and 85 percent of all churches in America have membership and attendance figures that have either plateaued or are declining. Churches are losing 2,765,000 people per year to nominal Christianity and outright unbelief. Between 3,500 and 4,000 churches die every year!

These statistics are sobering. For now, let us focus on the fact that little Escondido needs 133 new churches by A.D. 2000. Who will plant them? My denomination has an impressive vision for church planting, and it has excellent leadership and resources for its size in the field of home missions. Still, I don't expect that we will plant more than two churches per year in our presbytery (which includes not only San Diego

County, but also heavily populated Orange County, fast-growing
Riverside County, and the so-far sparsely populated Imperial County).
Who will plant the rest? Humanly speaking, the task is impossible; but
we pray that God will raise up church planters from many different
denominations to join in this great effort. No one denomination can do
it all; the labor must of necessity be cross-denominational.

That is why I no longer tremble when I hear rumors of another
church opening across the street from mine. If the new church is outward-facing, that is, if it is willing to put its major effort into carrying
out the Great Commission, we need not be rivals at all. Indeed, we
need one another. Another church in Escondido? We need 133!

On the other hand, if two churches are not outward-facing, they
can be threats to one another. If First Baptist is interested mainly in
nurturing Baptists rather than in reaching the unchurched, and a new
church (say, Calvary Baptist) appears on the next block, of course First
Baptist has a lot to worry about. Calvary Baptist may turn out to have
a more attractive minister, livelier programs for young people and the
like, so that some people might leave First Baptist to go there. And,
indeed, in that situation one might well criticize Calvary Baptist for
locating so close to another Baptist church. Far better, it seems, for
Calvary to find a location where there is now no Baptist witness.[7] But
consider that if First and Calvary were both outward-facing, they
would welcome one another's fellowship and assistance. Neither, most
likely, could share the gospel with *all* the unchurched in the town. If
both churches are evangelistically oriented, and God blesses their ministries, both could become large and successful in the eyes of God.

A Personal Evangelism Perspective

Another situation in which one's denominational chauvinism can be
broken down is personal evangelism. Let us say that you are dealing
with an unbelieving inquirer or a very young Christian who asks you
to recommend a church for him to attend. Naturally you would invite
him to your own congregation. But what if he lives in a different city,
distant enough that attending your church would be impractical?

Our first impulse is to recommend a church of our own denomination or of another denomination fairly similar to ours. But is that
always the best thing? In one city I know, there is a large evangelical
independent church with a dispensationalist pastor. The pastor is an
excellent communicator of the gospel and doesn't hammer much on
dispensational distinctives. He preaches mostly the positive teachings

of Scripture, communicates love for the lost and for fellow Christians of all backgrounds, while not being indifferent to what he regards as error. There is also in that city a Reformed church in a denomination closely related to my own. The Reformed pastor's theology is significantly closer to mine than that of the dispensationalist. But the Reformed man's sermons are exceedingly obscure and highly negative. The people of his congregation seem always to have chips on their shoulders, indignant about this or that; there is very little joy in the Lord, very little welcome to people of non-Reformed background. They claim to have much theological knowledge, but most of that "knowledge" is poorly thought out, often wrongly applied. The mentality in the church is very much inward-facing. Now, if I had only these two alternatives, which would I recommend to our inquirer? I would not hesitate to recommend the dispensationalist. To me the question is: In which congregation can my friend best hear the gospel and see its fruits? It is clear to me that the dispensationalist in my example *conveys far more of the truth* than the Reformed pastor.

This is not doctrinal indifference, but quite the reverse. I send my friend to the dispensationalist church because I know that he will there learn *more* sound doctrine, more authentic biblical content, than if he went to the church more confessionally similar to mine. My recommendation emerges out of my concern for sound doctrine; it is not a compromise of that concern.

This example is not based on unrealistic circumstances, since I have often had to give advice in similar situations. And when I look realistically at the needs of the inquirer and prayerfully consider the alternatives available, I see a better perspective and am often led beyond my own denomination, even my own theological tradition.

The Early Church

The final "perspective" I wish to place before you is that of the church in the first four centuries. It was certainly a church that was concerned with nurture. People were baptized and catechized; the believers sought to meet one another's material and spiritual needs. From the beginning, there was much doctrinal discussion and even controversy. The early church was not doctrinally indifferent; it mobilized against the Judaizers described in Galatians, the "antichrists" mentioned in 1 John 4, the later heresies of Sabellianism, Gnosticism, Marcionism, and Montanism.

At the same time, the early church would have to be described as

outward-facing. When the Christians were "scattered" (often by persecution), they "preached the word wherever they went" (Acts 8:4).
The *world* was always in the forefront of their thinking, in the nature
of the case. For it was an obvious battle in those days. The world was
intent on destroying the little church, and the little church was intent
on bringing the world to faith in Christ. I believe that God used this
self-understanding of the church to maintain its unity. For the
Christians were vitally aware of how much—in this life-and-death
struggle—they needed one another. The luxury of "churches made to
order" (denominations, in other words) was not a live option for most
of them. Novatian and Donatus were exceptions, but of course their
policy of rebaptism shows that they had the serious conviction that the
old church had apostatized, that it was no longer a church—a conviction rarely held or expressed by more recent founders of denominations. Schism, then, was possible in these early centuries, but only for
the gravest of reasons, reasons more serious than most any of those
given in modern times.

In the fourth century a Christian emperor came to the throne, and
the Roman Empire became nominally Christian. Many people joined
the church without much knowledge or conviction about its teachings, and understandably the focus of the church turned more inward,
though there were always some intrepid missionaries who continued
to introduce the gospel to new tribes and cultures. I cannot help,
however, connecting the relatively more inward-facing stance of the
church with the simultaneous trend toward more power politics and
excessive bickering within the church. That connection exists in a
number of inward-facing bodies that I have known and been a part of,
and I have no doubt that it is a universal connection. That trend is
certainly evident during the fourth-century Arian controversy and to a
much larger extent in the Christological controversies of the fifth century. Political maneuvering and/or resentment seems to be the major
reason why the Chalcedonian declaration of 451 was not approved by
the Egyptians and Syrians, who thus separated themselves from the
main body of believers. Similarly developed the great schism of 1054
between Eastern and Western churches and many (though not all) of
the subsequent denominational divisions.

Conclusion

The first step back to unity is to learn to see our denominational
differences in perspective. When we look at them from one angle, they

seem very important, very imposing, worthy of being maintained forever. From other angles (which, arguably, are more in accord with that of the Bible itself) they do not seem to be so great.

I have not established any specific conclusions in this chapter. There is nothing here, for example, that would motivate me to give up the Presbyterian confessions for my church to merge with a non-Presbyterian church. But much in this chapter does encourage me to look on other denominations—excluding, of course, cults, theological liberals, and other unbelievers masquerading as Christians—in a positive way, as friends rather than as enemies, as co-laborers in Christ. There is much here that influences me to listen to those friends with a more sympathetic and open mind, willing to be corrected even on matters my denomination considers to be settled.

I am convinced that such openness will in time be used of God to bring his church to a oneness beyond anything we have experienced in our day—a oneness not based on doctrinal indifference, but on a fuller understanding of God's word than any of our present groups can claim to have.

Notes

1. None of us is a "perfect" Calvinist.

2. See C. John Miller, *Outgrowing the Ingrown Church* (Grand Rapids: Ministry Resources Library, 1986).

3. The Great Commission itself, of course, requires nurture as well as evangelism—"teaching them to obey everything I have commanded you" (Matt. 28:20a).

4. *The Win Arn Growth Report* (Pasadena: 1986), p. 3.

5. Escondido's local reputation, by the way, is that it is "overchurched!"

6. Ibid., p. 3.

7. I confess I am not sure if there are any such locations! But bear with me for the sake of the illustration.

Dealing with
Doctrinal Differences

Doctrine divides, experience unites" is a common slogan today, but it is deeply misleading. No doubt there are many doctrinal disagreements in the church. Indeed, when we think of the reasons for continuing denominational divisions, we naturally think first of doctrinal differences. But we cannot brush doctrine aside as a mere impediment to unity, as many users of that slogan would like to do. A doctrinally indifferent church is a church that does not care about the gospel message; for the gospel is precisely a doctrine, a teaching, a narrative of what God has done for our salvation. Certainly any church worthy of the name must be doctrinally united, in the sense of being fully committed to one message, the gospel of Jesus Christ. It is this doctrine that unites us in our love for Christ; and it is our foolish trust in our own experience that leads us to compromise that message. Doctrine unites, experience divides![1]

What is this "gospel" to which we must all be committed? It is summarized in John 3:16; 5:24; Acts 2:38f; 16:31; Romans 3:23f; 1 Corinthians 15:3–8; Ephesians 2:8f; Titus 3:4–8; 1 Peter 3:18;

1 John 5:11f; and elsewhere. But the concepts in these verses are inti-mately related to those of other passages of Scripture, and they to still others, and so on. Our ultimate commitment, and the doctrinal basis of the church, is the entire Bible. It is not enough, however, for a church merely to confess the authority of Scripture. Many cults, for example, are doing that today, but they are certainly not preaching the authentic gospel of Christ. Therefore we must have in the church not only a common confession of biblical authority, but also some measure of common agreement as to what Scripture teaches.

In Defense of Tolerance

Note that I say "some measure." I do think it is unreasonable to require agreement on *every* doctrinal point within the church. It may well be doubted whether such total agreement can ever be achieved among human beings until the last judgment. To put the point that way is to make it seem obvious; most Christians would concede it. Sometimes, however, Christians talk as if total agreement were not only possible, but a prerequisite to fellowship: "The pretribulation rap-ture is God's truth! We may not compromise it! We must exclude any-one who denies it." This kind of talk makes sense only on the assump-tion that *everything* in Scripture is a test of orthodoxy, that no disagreement is to be tolerated on any matter. Once we agree that some toleration is legitimate, then certainly we cannot simply assume that the pretribulation rapture, or anything else, is a test of orthodoxy. Certainly, on that assumption, the mere fact that Scripture teaches a doctrine is insufficient to prove that that doctrine should be used as a test of orthodoxy. Those wishing to show that it is must offer addi-tional argument.

But why should there be toleration?[2] Even if we don't accept the pre-tribulation rapture, we can understand the point of those who would make it a test of fellowship. If God teaches the pretribulation rapture, who are we to deny it? And if the church is to guard God's truth, surely it must guard this truth also. Extending the argument, it would seem that the church must be totally agreed on every doctrinal matter.

Ah, but nobody really believes that. Even people who insist on uni-formity within the church as to pretribulationism generally allow for some areas of permissible disagreement. Every church I know of toler-ates disagreement on the reasons for God's rejecting Cain's sacrifice (Gen. 4:5), the meaning of the "mark" (Gen. 4:15), the exegesis of Genesis 6:1–4, the length of Israel's stay in Egypt (Exod. 12:40f; Acts

7:6), the reconciliation of the numbers in Kings and Chronicles, the nature of "baptism for the dead" (1 Cor. 15:29)[3] or of "sin unto death" (1 John 5:16). When you think about it, you can see that every denomination recognizes a great many teachings of Scripture about which sincere Christians may arrive at different conclusions.

Scripture itself explicitly warrants tolerance within certain limits. Of course, Scripture also speaks very strongly against heresy, false teaching. Those who preach "another gospel" are accursed (Gal. 1:6–9). Those who deny the resurrection eliminate the Christian hope (1 Cor. 15:1–34). Those denying the truth or teaching falsehood receive strong rebukes (2 Thess. 2; 3:14f; 1 Tim. 1:3ff; 6:3–5; 2 Tim. 2:14–19; 3:1–9; 4:3–5; Titus 3:9ff; 2 Peter 2; 3:4ff; 1 John 2:22f; 4:1–3; 2 John 7; Jude). God's people are urged to maintain the truth. But these instances of "false teaching" are all either denials of the basic gospel of grace, or else they are (as 1 Tim. 1:3ff) foolish speculations that distract us from Christ. These condemnations are not directed against merely incorrect opinions, as if every such incorrect opinion deserved condemnation. If that were true, we would all be condemned, for most likely we all hold some incorrect opinions. Indeed, some kinds of disagreements, such as the disagreement over idol food in 1 Corinthians 8, are *not* to result in anyone's condemnation, but in mutual forbearance (cf. Rom. 14; 15).

Here I must differ with Thomas M'Crie, whose defense of church unity I commended earlier in the present volume. M'Crie grants that some doctrines are more important than others, but then he adds:

> It is not, however, their comparative importance or utility, but their truth and the authority of him who has revealed [the doctrines], which is the proper and formal reason of our receiving, professing and maintaining them. And this applies equally to all the contents of a divine revelation.[4]

He continues:

> Whatever God has revealed we are bound to receive and hold fast; and whatever he has enjoined we are bound to obey; and the liberty which we dare not arrogate to ourselves we cannot give to others. It is not, indeed, necessary that the confession or testimony of the Church [meaning by this that which is explicitly made by her, as distinguished from her declared adherence to the whole Word of God] should contain all truths. But then any of them may come to be included in it, when opposed or endangered; and it is no sufficient reason for exclud-

ing any of them that they are less important than others, or that they have been doubted and denied by good and learned men.[5]

M'Crie evidently believes that once a consensus develops in a denomination over *any* biblical teaching, no matter how major or minor that teaching may be, the denomination may legitimately add that teaching to its confession of faith (though it is not obligated to do so) and thus prohibit any contrary views on pain of church discipline. Any doctrine, by that route, could become a test of orthodoxy. That could include interpretations of the sin unto death, baptism for the dead, or whatever.

I think that at this point M'Crie is simply wrong. For one thing, he ignores the fact that Scripture itself urges mutual tolerance in some areas of disagreement, as we have seen. On the basis of Romans 14, I would say that it would be very wrong for a denomination to forbid vegetarianism in its creed and subject vegetarians among its members to judicial penalties. The mere fact that God's word rejects the claims of the vegetarians is no reason to exercise formal sanctions against such people. M'Crie evidently fails to distinguish between our obligation to affirm what we think Scripture teaches (which includes the entire content of Scripture) and our obligation to exercise formal ecclesiastical discipline to test and maintain orthodoxy (an obligation that does not pertain to every teaching of Scripture). But that distinction is important; and if we observe it, there are some doctrinal differences that we may and must tolerate within the church, in the sense that those matters are not to be tests of orthodoxy.

I also reject the argument that says that since all biblical doctrines are interconnected—so that to reject one is implicitly to reject all the rest—therefore all must equally be regarded as tests of orthodoxy in the church. Surely there is a logical interconnection, though one may question how far it extends. To deny the deity of Christ, for example, logically entails (with a few other premises) a denial of the efficacy of the atonement. I doubt if any such momentous implications attach to one's view of baptism for the dead or (*contra* many) of the millennium. But even if there is a much tighter logical connection than I am able to see at the moment, the question still remains as to how much logical consistency is necessary to qualify one for church membership or church office. Logical consistency, after all, is something that is learned over time. Developing a logically consistent system of biblical doctrine is not a perfectly simple task; it has been the life work of some very great minds. It is an area in which most of us have some growing to do. To say that all doctrines of Scripture are tests of orthodoxy is to say that each church officer or even each member must have achieved such a system from the outset. Such a requirement seems to me to be obviously absurd and without any scriptural warrant. Indeed, even apostles were inconsistent at times (Gal. 2). Thus, we must accept the fact that Scripture permits doctrinal tolerance up to a point.

The Biblical Basis for Tolerance

Why does the Bible authorize this kind of tolerance?

1. *Scripture recognizes that each believer is subject to growth in his understanding*—and that even leaders in the church have some growing to do. That growth is a process; we may not demand that a church member or officer has all spiritual knowledge from the outset of his or her life or ministry. As it is with individuals, so it is with the church as a whole. Certainly God calls the church to guard all of his truth, "once for all entrusted to the saints" (Jude 3). But there are some areas in which the church simply cannot say it knows what that truth is! A study of history reveals that the church has grown very gradually in its understanding of Scripture. In every age, the church has been ignorant of important matters. In the first three centuries, formulations of the doctrine of the Trinity were accepted as orthodox, which after the fourth century would be universally rejected as heresy; likewise, doctrines of the person of Christ before Chalcedon. It is very difficult to find anyone before Luther who had a clear understanding of "justification by faith." And the church's understanding of "covenant" really began in the seventeenth century. Is it not possible that we, too, are ignorant of some matters that future generations of Christians (or perhaps no one before the *eschaton*) will come to understand? If so, it would make sense to tolerate various opinions in these areas[6] until the church is able to reach a unity of mind. In my view the church in the year 200 would have been wrong to require of its ministers a fully wrought-out understanding of the Trinity, even if the proposed formulation happened to be right. For there was at that time no consensus. There had not been sufficient clear teaching in the church on this subject so that those deviating from a norm could be charged with rebelliousness. Although the doctrine of the Trinity was in the Bible, there was a sense in which, as of A.D. 200, God had not *taught* that doctrine to the church.

2. *Scripture also recognizes that there are different levels of difficulty within God's revelation itself.* Even Peter says that Paul's letters contain things that are hard to be understood (2 Peter 3:16).[7] The biblical

requirements for church membership, even for the eldership, do not include intellectual brilliance. It may very well be, as Cornelius Van Til argues, that the doctrine of the Trinity resolves the philosophical question of the One and the Many; but it would be wrong for a church to require its members or elders to understand, confess, or endorse that proposition.

3. *Another factor that somewhat limits our understanding of the Bible is the cultural and historical distance between ourselves and the biblical period.* On the general level, there is our ignorance of biblical languages, customs, and so on. More specifically, it is clear that the readers of 1 Corinthians, for example, knew some things that we don't know and are not likely to find out. This epistle is evidently a response to a letter that the church wrote to Paul. The Corinthians may have remembered the precise contents of that letter; we can never do that. The Corinthians evidently knew what "baptism for the dead" was. We are not in their position. The same logic pertains to doctrinal issues like infant baptism. In the first century, that problem was easily solved. If anyone had a question, he could simply look up the nearest apostle and inquire as to the apostolic practice. We cannot do that. Nor, since the Reformation, do we acknowledge any single source as an accurate transmitter of apostolic tradition.

4. *Another reason for tolerance is that some matters in Scripture* (pace *M'Crie) are just not important enough to be used as tests of orthodoxy.* Here we must be careful: for who are we to declare something in God's word unimportant? Yet the Lord himself distinguishes between weightier and less weighty matters in God's revelation (Matt. 23:23). We are speaking here not of absolute importance but of *relative* importance (i.e., compared to other teachings of God's Word). And we are seeking to determine that importance not by subjecting Scripture to our autonomous standards, but by comparing Scripture with Scripture, by listening to what Scripture itself takes to be important. Baptism for the dead, even if we do come to understand what it is, is not central enough in Scripture, not closely enough connected to the central message of Scripture, to be a test of orthodoxy.

Now I think God understands all this (pardon the understatement). He knows that there are levels of importance in Scripture and that we are historically removed from the scriptural milieu through no fault of our own. He knows that Scripture is difficult at points and that growth in knowledge is a process. He does not, therefore, expect either church members or officers to know and affirm specifically every teaching of Scripture. And if he does not expect this, neither must we demand it. There must be some room for different opinions on matters in which these factors play a role.

When a church teacher holds to a respectable interpretation of, say, the "sin unto death," which we personally believe to be erroneous, we generally do not (and should not) conclude that this error disqualifies him as a teacher. We are still free to regard him as sound and edifying. Indeed, on such matters, most of us would concede the strong possibility that we *might* be wrong (even if we sincerely believe we are right) and that the teacher in question might be right. That would not be the case if, say, in my PCA church this person taught a Roman Catholic view of justification.[8]

What Views Are Tolerable?

We must ask seriously what doctrinal differences should be tolerated in the church today. That is a difficult question to answer, contrary to those who assume without argument that, for example, the pretribulation rapture must be a test of orthodoxy. It is difficult, first, because to my knowledge no one has ever studied the question in a truly systematic way. Many have asked which doctrines are true; few (if any) have asked from distinctively evangelical premises[9] how much diversity the church ought to tolerate.

Second, the question is difficult to answer because the answer is historically variable. If my earlier argument is correct, views tolerable in the church in the year 200 are not necessarily tolerable in the year 2000, since God continually teaches his church new things out of the Scriptures.

Third, the question is particularly difficult because of the scourge of denominationalism. The more divided the church is, the less able it is to study the Scriptures *together*. The great trinitarian formulations of Nicaea and Constantinople were the fruit of discussion throughout the entire church (even the Novatianists and the Donatists were not totally excluded from the dialog). But as the church became more divided, the developing of a church-wide consensus became more and more difficult. Adversary relationships among denominations led Christians to take less seriously the theological developments in other denominations. Lutherans rarely learned from Calvinists, or Catholics from Anabaptists, or Independents from Eastern Orthodox. Young theologians growing up in these traditions have been hardened against serious consideration of other positions by hearing constant polemics and by having little firsthand knowledge of the other views. From

God's point of view, the situation may be described thus: God has been teaching different denominations at different rates.

When study of "covenant" began in earnest in the seventeenth century, it was largely limited to Reformed circles. Now, three centuries later, we are seeing the fruit of that study in many denominations. Most all theologians today admit that "covenant" is a central category of biblical theology. We can be thankful for that process; but my guess is that had the church been united, the dissemination of this knowledge would have taken much less time.

There are signs that some in the Roman Catholic Church are rethinking, sympathetically this time, the doctrine of justification by faith. Personally, I am delighted that this is happening, but I very much regret that it could not have happened four hundred years ago.

Part of the problem is the imbalance of gifts from one denomination to another. Some denominations may have an overabundance of scholarly and spiritual theological talent, and so they learn God's lessons at a faster rate.[10] Other denominations may be gifted in other ways, but slower to learn theological doctrines. Another part of the problem may be that God teaches different things to different denominational groups. He has taught Polish Catholics and Chinese Christians many things about dealing with the gospel's adversaries that he has not taught the rest of us. God taught the Roman Catholics about the terrible evil of abortion long before that concern took hold within Protestant evangelicalism. At present, East African Christians seem to have had much more experience with, and insight into, revival than have Christians living elsewhere.

The tolerance I advocate should not be confused with doctrinal indifference. My argument is not that doctrine in general is unimportant or that the church should tolerate an unlimited number of different views. Nor do I think tolerance is good in itself, an attitude to be cultivated in all church matters. Rather, even the amount of tolerance I advocate is based on our *limitations*, which we hope to overcome as God gives wisdom and strength. The ideal is not a tolerant church where all views are given equal respect (i.e., doctrinal indifference); rather, it is a church where all members are agreed on the truth so that tolerance of opposing views is unnecessary. We have not reached that ideal yet, and we may not reach it until we are in heaven. At the present stage of history, there must be tolerance simply because there is no alternative.

Back to the Future?

In an earlier draft of this book, I suggested what I called my "back to the future" proposal, which would involve uniting all Christians under one church government doctrinally based on the Scriptures and the Nicene-Constantinopolitan Creed of A.D. 381. That creed was the last creed agreed to by the one, true church and is acknowledged by virtually all Christians to this day. That would, in effect, take us back before 451, before the major schisms. Then we could study Scripture together, hopefully without the atmosphere of party spirit, time pressure, and fear that has surrounded such discussions in the past.

The assumption of the proposal is that—since God has been teaching different denominations at different rates—each group should be willing to wait, in effect, for the others to catch up. For example, Presbyterians should seek to teach their view of predestination to the whole church, so that the whole church could pass judgment on it, before that doctrine is given creedal status.

This proposal, I think, would not be disastrous for the church. As I indicated earlier, the church existed for 300 years before agreeing on a definitive formulation of the doctrine of the Trinity. Similarly, 450 years for Christology, 1,500 years for an adequate formulation of justification by faith, still longer for an adequate doctrine of predestination. Yet, during these waiting periods, churches were being planted, souls saved, believers taught, the poor cared for. After all, people can come to salvation with very little if any intellectual grasp of theology. People can be saved (i.e., justified by predestinating grace through faith) without being able to *articulate* the doctrines in view. Someone who trusts Christ exclusively and entirely for forgiveness and salvation surely belongs to Christ, whether or not that person is able to articulate the nature of that trust.[11]

However, even in the previous draft I had to admit that this proposal is not a very practical one. The chances of our agreeing to accept it are very slight indeed, and if we did accept it, we would still have a lot of growing to do before we could listen to one another without the antagonisms of our denominational past. I merely mention it to indicate some of the issues that would have to be considered if reunion is our goal.

And, to be honest, I must say that I really do not want to endorse the proposal, even in principle. I really do not want to be part of a church that is unwilling to subscribe to the New Testament doctrines of justification and predestination. In this modern period, attempts to preach the gospel without acknowledging those scriptural truths are confusing. We can do much better than that, for God has taught some of us how. I would not want to be in a church where, for even a while, ministers were free to disagree with these teachings. These truths are too precious to be lost in an ecumenical shuffle. Their loss would not be a disaster, as I said earlier, but it would be crippling in the present context. Perhaps I am here admitting that I am not as ecumenical as I claim to be. If so, may God teach me a better way. But I am sure that reunion worthy of the name will not appear on a basis of doctrinal indifference, but on a basis of greater doctrinal insight, granted by God to the whole church.

Another argument against "back to the future" is the existence of theological liberalism in many denominations today. As I have said earlier, I believe, with many evangelicals, that liberalism (in its many forms, including "neo-orthodoxy") is not Christianity, but another, humanistic religion expressed in Christian language. Any worthwhile proposal for reunion would need at the same time to exclude liberal elements. But, if we adopted the "back to the future" proposal, I suspect that many liberals would join in. The Nicene-Constantinopolitan Creed, to be sure, is supernaturalistic enough to exclude liberalism; but I doubt if it is sufficiently detailed to refute the subtleties of language that liberals use to conceal the radicalism of their theology.

I raise the "back to the future" proposal, therefore, not as a serious plan for reunion, but as a way to stimulate our thinking toward a more practical plan. Though I do not wish to tolerate those who deny justification by faith or biblical predestination, there may be room for tolerance on some other matters that we often take for granted. Perhaps it is impractical to suggest that we all merge into one church, aware of contested issues, and then study the Scriptures together with a view to solving the disagreements. But surely, at the very least, we ought to promote cross-denominational Bible study in all of these areas. Such Bible study should avoid partisanship and political maneuvering; it should be hemmed on all sides by a spirit of love, gentleness, teachability. Do I believe that we can thereby make some progress on issues that have been contested for hundreds of years? By God's grace, yes, I do.

There will be some more specific practical proposals in the final chapter of this book. Practical steps are not my strong suit, however. What I hope to do in this book is to communicate a vision to others who can implement that vision far more effectively than I can. Hence a few more "perspectives" follow.

Perspectivalism in Doctrine

As we seek to engage fellow Christians in cross-denominational dialog, it is important to keep in mind certain fundamental facts about
the Scriptures and about theology. For one thing, Scripture itself is a
wonderfully rich and many-faceted book. It does not fit the pattern
that has become stereotyped in our systematic theologies. Rather, it
contains narrative, poetry, wisdom literature, apocalyptic, law, epistle.
Within those books are many types of language: indicatives, impera-
tives, interrogatives, performatives, treaties, parables, exclamations, literal, figurative, allusive, vague, precise, solemn, humorous, denuncia-
tion, encouragement, general, specific, and so on.

Teachings of Scripture, or "doctrines," are found in various places
in Scripture and are learned in various ways. Sometimes they are stated
fairly straightforwardly, as in Paul's epistles. However, we must
remember that Paul does not (even in Romans) intend to write what
we would call a systematic theology. He is dealing with the needs of
particular churches. The doctrinal truths of Paul's letters must be carefully extracted, to make sure we are rightly applying his "occasional"
thoughts to our general theological questions. In other parts of
Scripture, we need to use even more exegetical caution. Narrative
teaches doctrine, but it does so in a different way from parable or epistle or wisdom literature. Many doctrinal disagreements arise out of
failure (by one party or both) to exegete carefully, taking into account
the sort of language found in Scripture.

It is also interesting to note another form of richness in Scripture:
God seems to delight in teaching the same thing in many different
ways. He gives us two accounts of the kings of Judah: one in Samuel–
Kings, the other in Chronicles. He gives us four accounts of Jesus'
earthly ministry, death, and resurrection: the four Gospels. He gives us
a prose account of the Red Sea crossing (Exod. 12–14) and a poetic
account (Exod. 15, but also several Psalms). The doctrine of faith
appears in the life of Abraham, in the epistles of Paul, in Hebrews 11,
in James 2. Truths about the nature of God are repeated under different symbolic portrayals: God as warrior, as shepherd, as king, as artisan
(creator), as wisdom teacher, as deliverer, as nurse, and so on. Similarly
for Christ, for salvation, for the nature of the church.

Why all this repetition? Well, it isn't really repetition; for each time
Scripture "repeats" something, it gives fresh illumination. It presents
the old truth from a new angle. In one sense, the whole biblical message is presented in Genesis 3:15. But God was not satisfied to leave

us with only that early formulation of the Good News. He wanted us to explore its aspects, to meditate, to see it from many angles.

These "angles" I am in the habit of calling "perspectives." As in my earlier use of the term in this book, a perspective is a viewpoint on something. Since we are finite beings and cannot see everything at once as God can, it is important that we at least see the truth from as many different perspectives, or angles, as we can. In an earlier book, I went into some detail as to the bearing of this principle on theology.[12] Here let me simply say that it is especially important to multiply perspectives when we are discussing doctrine cross-denominationally.

We should at least consider the possibility that some doctrinal differences are the result of two parties coming to the scriptural text from different perspectives. I think that the seventeenth-century controversy between supra- and infra-lapsarians is certainly a controversy of this sort.[13] I would not say that all doctrinal differences can be described that way, since certainly the more serious divisions are not *mere* differences in perspective. Rather, in most of these controversies, one or both parties is simply in error.[14] Still, in most of these controversies, there is an element of perspectival difference as well as elements of error. For example, surely the Arminian comes to the question of predestination with a different focus from the Calvinist's. He is interested primarily in maintaining human responsibility and freedom. The Calvinist, on the other hand, is interested more in maintaining the sovereignty of God. Both concerns are scriptural; one might say they are both legitimate perspectives from which to view the issues. Combine this perspectival difference with a difference (somewhere) of truth versus error, and you have a debate on your hands.

Vern Poythress recommends, and I concur, that in situations like this we try to "pre-empt" the other person's fundamental concerns. Rather than going on and on about the sovereignty of God, the Calvinist should seek to show that his view does better justice to human responsibility and freedom. The Arminian should seek to show that his view results in a credible doctrine of divine sovereignty. I do believe that we will be more likely to see our own errors if we make an effort to consider the issues from the perspectives of others. Certainly this is required if we are to show biblical love for one another in the process of theological discussion. And certainly we will maximize our understanding of Scripture if we are able to see the same truth from a maximum number of perspectives.

Subscription

Creeds, I believe, are a valid and important way for churches to present to the world their understanding of the biblical message.[15] A denomination rightly exerts theological discipline by requiring some allegiance to these standards. But there have been many kinds of subscription through history. One may distinguish subscription by officers from subscription by all church members, subscription to every "jot and tittle" of the creed from a more general subscription to the system of doctrine found in the creed, and so on.

In my view, only a very minimal subscription should be required of church members in general. The conditions for church membership should be no narrower than the Scriptures' conditions for belonging to the kingdom of God. Anyone who can make a credible profession of faith in Christ should be welcomed into the church (together, I must add as a paedobaptist, with his/her children). "Credible profession" is not a precise concept. It should normally involve[16] the willingness to confess that Jesus is one's own Lord and Savior: that Jesus, who is both God and man, died for the sins of his people to bring them forgiveness, and that he now has full authority over our lives as the resurrected, living Lord (cf. the biblical summaries of the gospel mentioned at the beginning of this chapter). Of course, it is quite proper to determine through questioning the extent to which a person really understands what he is saying; but it would surely be wrong to assume that no one can make a credible profession without mastering Hodge's *Systematic Theology*. It is also proper to examine the life of a candidate for church membership, at least enough to determine if it is consistent with his profession of faith. But it should not be necessary to point out that such an examination must be satisfied with far less than perfection. A profession of faith is a claim to follow Jesus, not a claim to have reached our ultimate destination.

Some groups have argued that because a church must be unified in its confession, every member of that church should be expected to subscribe to the church's doctrinal standards. But in churches with fairly elaborate doctrinal standards (such as the Westminster Confession of Faith or the Heidelberg Catechism), this sort of policy would restrict church membership to the highly intelligent, for only they are capable of intelligently subscribing to such documents. This would be a very narrow criterion, far narrower than that of Scripture itself.[17] Lack of such a policy need not bring disunity. A congregation is united by its faith, not by its intelligence. And there is no reason why a congregation might not leave the more important decisions in the hands of those who do subscribe to its standards, so that the lack of universal subscription would not lead to any deterioration in its commitment.

Among church officers, it is legitimate to expect them to subscribe to confessional statements, for the issue with them is not their faith as such (as in the case of members), but their qualifications to teach and make decisions for the church. Even here, however, we must be careful what form the subscription takes. If the church requires its officers to subscribe to every "jot and tittle" of the confession on pain of ecclesiastical discipline, the confession becomes in principle unamendable.[18] Anyone wishing to amend it would on that very account be subject to discipline. An unamendable creed becomes, in effect, the equivalent of Scripture; Scripture itself loses its unique authority in the church. There must be some leeway, some at least momentary tolerance, some leg room for people who conscientiously believe that something in the confession is unscriptural. The arrangement may be forcing the church into a reexamination of its doctrines, or on less important matters (see earlier discussion) it might simply lead to permitting differences in these areas.

We ought to do some more thinking about what doctrines really are nonnegotiable. The Evangelical Free Church requires professors at Trinity Evangelical Divinity School to hold a premillennial eschatology, but it permits latitude on the differences between Calvinists and Arminians. In my view that indicates a rather large overestimation of the importance of millennial views and a large underestimation of the importance of the doctrine of predestination. But perhaps I am wrong. The whole question of what is and what is not tolerable within the church has never been systematically analyzed.

As we do such analysis, it should be with a view to the effect it will have on a biblical ecumenism. Obviously, the more "nonnegotiable" doctrines we have, the more difficult it will be to merge our own denomination with other bodies. And the stricter our formula of subscription, the more difficult it will be to enter organizational union with other churches. Of course, it is more important to be biblical than to be maximally available for church unions. But ecumenism is also a biblical goal, and it may work to help keep us from needlessly overcommitting ourselves in areas where Scripture allows some tolerance of diversity.

Notes

1. I admit I am being a little cute here. A more balanced perspective is that *true* doctrine unites, and *genuine* experience of God through the Spirit of Christ also unites. Distortions on either side lead to division. And a simple factual analysis of the situation will show that both doctrine (e.g., the

Calvinist doctrine of predestination) and "experience" (e.g., the charismatic experiences of tongues and prophecy) can become items of disagreement by which churches are divided. One may recognize that without making any assumption about the validity of the doctrine or experience at issue.

2. There are two questions here. One is: What can be tolerated within the membership of the church? and the other: What can be tolerated among the official teachers of the church? In what follows, I am thinking primarily of the second question. The first is also important, but I think it can be dealt with in parallel ways. Of course, our answers to the two questions will not necessarily be the same.

3. Mormonism has a very definite doctrine about "baptism for the dead." That is one of the things that makes Mormonism a cult, rather than a church.

4. Thomas M'Crie, *The Unity of the Church* (Dallas, Tex.: Presbyterian Heritage Publications, 1989), p. 110.

5. Ibid., p. 111.

6. Within some limits, of course. If someone thinks the "sin unto death" is jaywalking, I would question his competence as an exegete. If he thinks the "sin unto death" is joining the PCA, I would suspect something seriously wrong with his theology.

7. This fact does not conflict with the Protestant confession of the *clarity* of Scripture. "Clarity" in this context simply means that the way of salvation in Scripture is plain enough to be understood by unlearned people as well as by scholars. I would add the provision that Scripture is "clear" in such a way that we may never blame our disobedience on its relative obscurities. But it is not necessarily clear enough to give every reader an instantaneous, fully adequate, systematic theology.

8. Even here it is theoretically possible that we could be wrong; but the pervasiveness and central importance of justification by faith in the New Testament leads us to give it a presuppositional status. See my *Doctrine of the Knowledge of God* (Phillipsburg, N.J.: Presbyterian and Reformed), pp. 134ff.

9. Liberals have, of course, written much in support of theological tolerance. This is mainly tolerance of liberal ideas; they have not, characteristically, urged their churches to tolerate ideas that they stigmatize as fundamentalist. But their accounts are largely unacceptable to evangelicals because they presume an indifference to doctrine, an indifference to what we regard as God's revealed truth.

10. Am I being presumptuous if I state my feeling (or prejudice) that such is the case in my own, Reformed, branch of the church? By the way, I do see this as a mixed blessing, for in my view the Reformed community would probably be better off with fewer intellectuals and more people with other sorts of gifts.

11. I am helped here also by my Reformed conviction that infants can be regenerate. They would be even clearer examples of such "inarticulate" faith. I realize that not all evangelicals would accept this doctrine, but I suggest they consider the implications of 2 Samuel 12:23; Ps. 51:5; Luke 1:15, 44; and Acts 2:39 in their contexts.

12. J. Frame, *Doctrine of the Knowledge of God*. See also Vern Poythress, *Symphonic Theology* (Grand Rapids: Zondervan, 1987).

13. See ibid., pp. 264ff.

14. Note that perspectivalism is not relativism.

15. See J. Frame, *Doctrine of the Knowledge of God*, pp. 225f, 304–310.

16. I say "normally" to set aside cases of severe mental retardation, people without hearing or speech, and so on.

17. Donald Macleod points out that "The three thousand converts at Pentecost, the Ethiopian Chancellor and the Philippian Jailer were certainly not indoctrinated to the level of the Three Forms of Unity" ("Ecumenism: Lessons from Vancouver '89," *Outlook* [Dec. 1989]: 15–18; quote from 16). The "Three Forms of Unity" are the Belgic Confession, the Heidelberg Catechism and the Canons of Dordt, which are the usual doctrinal standards of Reformed churches in Europe.

18. At least unamendable by subtraction; it could be amended by addition, or by a change that leaves all its present doctrinal commitments intact.

9

• • • • • • • • • • • • • • • • • • • •

Dealing with Differences in Practice

The contrast between "doctrine" and "practice" comes readily to the minds and lips of church people, as roughly the equivalent of the common theoretical/practical distinction. The *Westminster Shorter Catechism* identifies the content of Scripture as beliefs and duties (Q., A. 3) and then bases its own two-part structure on that contrast. Sometimes the basic idea is put as a distinction between "faith" and "life."

At best this contrast is only a rough, general one. Many matters are hard to classify on one side or the other of the distinction. What about the sacraments, for instance? Indeed, the actual beliefs, or doctrines, of Christians are revealed in their actions as well as in their words; practices are ways of expressing doctrines. Conversely, doctrines emerge out of practices—ultimately from the deeds of God, Jesus, and the apostles, proximately from the behavior of Christians that influences their doctrinal formulations. Therefore, most of the considerations mentioned in the previous chapter apply here as well. In "practice" also, Scripture warrants tolerance of differences within certain limits, and we ought to apply that tolerance (carefully observing the limits) to maximize unity.

But, without getting into heavy epistemology, I will here use the familiar distinction as a very rough tool, to make some sense out of the relation of this to the previous chapter.

Obviously I will not be able to deal here with *all* the practices of the church, which would require omniscience. However, I shall deal with some of the more important ones that have historically been barriers to church union. That a church practice inhibits church union does not necessarily make it a bad practice. Rather, such a practice needs to be considered to see if it can be carried on in such a way as not to discourage unity.

Sacraments

Certainly among the most important practices in the church are the sacraments, about which there are many differences among the denominations. Disagreements exist as to the definition of a sacrament, how many there are, the subjects to which they should be administered, who is entitled to administer them, what constitutes "valid" sacraments, what procedures are correct, what the sacraments symbolize, what they "seal," how Christ is "present" in them. Many of these issues are doctrinal and fall under the observations of chapter 6. Let me here discuss a few additional matters that cause problems for unity.

Baptism

Are Differences over the Subjects of Baptism Tolerable?

It is sometimes said, for example, that Presbyterians and Baptists can never unite because they differ on the subjects of baptism and therefore would differ as to the membership of the church. This is a significant question, because there are Baptists who agree fully with Reformed theology and even with Presbyterian government, except on this one subject. I did say earlier that church membership is an important matter, a way by which an individual believer can be put under the oversight of a particular body of elders as the New Testament requires. Thus the idea of a "membership roll" is a legitimate one. The question is, however, whether that roll must be absolutely precise. Surely it would not be a breach of decency and order if a Presbyterian church were to merge with a Baptist church and keep a roll of members "and their children," leaving open (i.e., tolerating a difference as to) the actual status of these children, and allowing each family (or each congregation within a denomination) to practice its own convictions as to whether or not the children should be baptized.[1]

I do believe in infant baptism myself; I think it can be proved from Scripture.[2] But the argument for it is somewhat difficult, and I can readily sympathize with fellow believers who don't agree with me on this point. The debate could have been easily resolved in the first century by reference to the apostolic practice. But many years have gone by since that time, and during the Reformation the Protestants and Anabaptists came to distrust the claims of the Roman Catholic Church to transmit the apostolic practice without distortion. Whether that distrust was right or wrong, it made the question far more difficult than it otherwise would have been. All in all, I would encourage union between Baptist and Presbyterian bodies that are otherwise agreed, allowing for diverse opinions on the subjects of baptism.

Are Baptisms by Other Denominations Valid?

Another problem is in determining the validity of baptisms from outside one's own denomination.[3] The early church took a rather liberal view on this subject. Augustine argued that the church should recognize the baptisms of schismatics and heretics, and his view did prevail, though it has been questioned by many since his time.

There are some today who accept the validity of only those baptisms performed within their own denomination. For shame! That view seems to me to represent the epitome of denominationalism, and denominationalism at its worst. It is a view without any basis in Scripture, one that elevates particular denominations far beyond their legitimate status, and that in effect denies the existence of true faith beyond its own organization, thereby insulting the whole body of Christ.

My view is that when a person claims to have been baptized, showing a fairly knowledgeable understanding of the theology of baptism, we should take his word for it unless we have evidence to the contrary. That is to say, the burden of proof is on those who would show that his claim is false. To deny someone's claim to have been baptized is essentially an act of discipline. And discipline in Scripture, like American civil law, follows the principle of "innocent until proved guilty." In biblical terms, the principle is "two or three witnesses" (Deut. 17:6; 19:15; Matt. 18:16; 2 Cor. 13:1; 1 Tim. 5:19)—that is, if you want to prove that someone is guilty, you must make a strong case. In the absence of such a strong case, you dare not accuse someone of wrongdoing.

What might constitute evidence of invalid baptism? That might in itself be matter for disagreement among Christians. The individual church or denomination would have to decide; but acknowledging the

burden of proof as I have suggested will necessarily lead them to accept
claims to baptism in most situations, and that will be favorable to unity.
But they might choose to recognize as evidence of invalid baptism, for
example, evidence that the "church" that performed the baptism had
repudiated the gospel and therefore had no right to baptize anyone.[4]

"Fencing the Table"

Related questions arise in connection with the Lord's Supper. The
apostle Paul tells us that "A man ought to examine himself before he
eats of the bread and drinks of the cup. For anyone who eats and
drinks without recognizing the body of the Lord eats and drinks judgment on himself. That is why many among you are weak and sick, and
a number of you have fallen asleep" (1 Cor. 11:28–30). Interpreters
differ as to the nature of the sin here described as "not recognizing
the body of the Lord." It is plain, however, that this sin has serious
consequences, so serious that those who may be guilty of it are best
advised not to take the bread and cup. To protect people from these
serious consequences, many churches have made some attempt to
restrict the sacrament to those who can reasonably be expected to partake worthily (cf. v. 27). These attempts are sometimes called "fencing
the table." Sometimes this consists only of a warning from the pulpit.
Other times the officer(s) of the congregation physically withhold the
sacrament from those who, in the governing body's opinion, are by
doctrine or lifestyle not worthy partakers.

Who may take communion? In some congregations, only members
of that congregation in good standing (*closed* communion). That plays
it safe with 1 Corinthians 11:27–30. In some other congregations,
communion is restricted to members in good standing plus others
who can give evidence of their good standing elsewhere. Sometimes
"elsewhere" is restricted to the denomination in question; sometimes
it is more broadly applied. The so-called evidence is, in some cases, a
letter from one's home church; in other cases it may be one's own testimony. These approaches are sometimes called *restricted* communion.
Open communion exists where the minister presiding at communion
gives a warning,[5] but leaves it up to each worshiper whether or not he
or she will partake. Sometimes the minister's remarks will recommend
participation only by those who are members in good standing of
Christian or evangelical churches.

Open communion certainly permits members of different churches
or denominations to have maximum access to one another's communion tables. In that sense it promotes unity and therefore ought to be

preferred if it can be shown to be a scriptural procedure. I believe it *is* scriptural. Note that:

1. 1 Corinthians 11 puts the responsibility for taking communion worthily entirely on the individual: "A man ought to *examine himself.* . . . But *if we judged ourselves,* we would not come under judgment" (vv. 28, 31, emphasis added).
2. Elders in the church have only spiritual, not physically coercive power. They may exhort, but they are not, like the civil government, given the power of the sword. They may give advice and often should, but they may not physically prevent people from taking communion.
3. Only open communion preserves the biblical judicial principle of "innocent until proven guilty," as discussed above. If people hear the warning and claim—by taking the elements—that they are fit to receive communion, the church is obligated to accept their testimony unless it has strong reasons for believing otherwise.[6]

Worship

The sacraments are part of worship, of course, but let us now look at worship from a more general viewpoint. In present-day America, the church is in ferment concerning worship styles. Many different approaches are found, all arguing their scripturality and competing for the allegiance of Christians. Differences over worship are certainly one source of disunity within the church today.

I hope sometime to write a book on worship that will argue (as you might expect) that Scripture permits a fairly wide range of approaches and styles. We cannot go into all the arguments now. Suffice it to say that although one can show various advantages in, say, formal liturgical worship, it is impossible to show that Scripture *requires* this as the *exclusive* mode of worship for God's people. The same can be said for the other common alternatives.

If we grant this conclusion, I believe that we will have to consider a wide variety of matters in determining how we shall worship. One of those is, again, our concern for church unity. There are some kinds of worship that tend to be exclusive, where congregations do various things that are not well understood outside their churches and/or their denominations. The impact of this sort of thing on visitors is not beneficial. I have visited churches where the members regularly stand, sit, kneel, at various points of the service, but where there is no way a visitor can gain information as to what to do and when. Sometimes the members are little or no help to the visitor, and the visitor feels left out.

Worship ought to be conducted in a welcoming atmosphere. No one should be made to feel out of place, by his clothing, his poverty (James 2:1–13; cf. 1 Cor. 11:22), his race (Gal. 2:11–14; Eph. 2:11–22), or, presumably, his inexperience in the tradition of the church. In worship, too, love of the brethren must abound.[7]

In my view, these considerations favor an informal type of worship, in which most everything is explained to visitors, and in which the music and language are simple and fairly familiar in style. However, these arguments do not necessarily rule out other kinds of worship. I have been in formal liturgical services where the various activities were clearly outlined for visitors and where the congregation was exceedingly hospitable.

Other practices that reinforce denominational divisions and inhibit the growth of unity will be discussed in succeeding chapters. The moral here is that we ought to take the unity of the church into account when we discuss ways of doing things in the church. Often, I think, we tend to plan our church activities without even thinking about the bearing of these activities on unity. I pray that God will eliminate that dullness from our hearts.

Notes

1. *Alternatives:* (1) Allowing the decision to be made by the individual congregation, so that each presbytery or convention would include churches of both convictions. Or (2) Allowing, say, Baptist and non-Baptist presbyteries within an overall Presbyterian denomination.

2. See John Murray, *Christian Baptism* (Philadelphia: Presbyterian and Reformed, 1952).

3. Similar questions arise as to the recognition of ministerial ordination.

4. Of course, formal judgments by one church that another church is totally apostate have been exceedingly rare in church history. Augustine did not make such a judgment against the schismatics and heretics of his day; the Protestant Reformers did not make it against the Roman Catholic Church; the Puritans did not so judge the Anglican Church, nor did J. Gresham Machen so condemn the Presbyterian Church, U.S.A.

5. Sometimes, to be sure, there is not even a warning. That is also open communion, but I do not favor it. A minister does have a responsibility at least to warn worshipers of spiritual danger.

6. When it has such a strong reason, as when an excommunicated person known to the elders seeks to take the sacrament, the elders ought to engage in some additional and fervent pleading, but nothing more.

7. It simply is not true, pious as it may sound, that in worship we must concentrate on God alone. Scripture requires of us even in worship to care for one another in love.

10

Dealing with Historical Differences

By "historical" I am referring not only to the doctrinal and practical differences discussed in the previous two chapters, though certainly those, too, are historical in a sense. Rather, I am talking about various historical events that have created barriers to union.

Historic Animosities

Many denominations dwell on the injustices that have been done against them by other denominations. Often, for instance, new denominations have originated because an older denomination disciplined some of its members in ways considered unfair by those members (and their sympathizers). The mutual excommunications of the Roman Pope and the Patriarch of Constantinople remain barriers to reunion of two great branches of the church. The discipline of Luther by the Roman Church, of J. Gresham Machen by the Presbyterian Church, U.S.A., and of Klaas Schilder by the Reformed Churches in the Netherlands continue to be barriers to reunion of those bodies with the bodies founded by their former members. Sometimes, too, people have left a denomination without formal discipline, for reasons greatly resented by the original body, such as in the split between Bible Presbyterians and Orthodox Presbyterians in 1937.

Even more serious are the literal religious wars that have taken place over the years. French Protestants will never forget the St. Bartholomew's Day Massacre of 1572 in which at least 30,000 Huguenots were slain. And can Irish Protestants and Catholics ever forget the "troubles" that still poison their relationships today?

Emotional hurts and resentments are among the most difficult hindrances to reunion. From a biblical perspective, however, certain things are clear:

1. The children are not to be punished for the sins of the fathers (Ezek. 18:1–24). For example, we are not to hold later generations of Roman Catholics guilty for the great crime of the St. Bartholomew's Day Massacre.
2. Forgiveness is to be liberal (Matt. 18:21ff).
3. We should not dwell on our hurts and on past evils, but on those things that are "true . . . noble . . . right . . . pure . . . lovely . . . admirable" (Phil. 4:8a).
4. Bodies that originate in schism, however bitter the circumstances, may nevertheless deserve our respect as true churches, as Augustine recognized the validity of Donatist baptism.
5. People and denominations change. Groups that were sharply at odds with one another fifty years ago may be very close together today, but without recognizing it. It is important to focus on the *present* situation in determining our relationships with other bodies.

Ethnicity

The Reformed Church of America and the Presbyterian Church, U.S.A. were largely the same in doctrine when they were founded (in 1628 and 1706 respectively). They differed mainly in that the former was Dutch in origin, the latter Scottish. Today also there are many denominations (especially in multi-ethnic nations like the United States) whose main reason for separate existence seems to be their ethnic constituency. This would be true of the Christian Reformed Church (Dutch), the Evangelical Free Church (Norwegian-Danish), the Evangelical Covenant Church (Swedish), the Reformed Church,

U.S. (German), the Korean-American Presbyterian Church (Korean), the Church of God in Christ (African-American), and others.

Nor should we allow our white Anglo-Saxon churches to get off the hook at this point. For they, too, consist largely of one ethnic group, and those churches also serve as refuges from the multicultural world where one can be with his "own people."

Although I do not believe Scripture requires every congregation to be multi-ethnic, I do believe that every congregation is to *welcome* visitors regardless of race, ethnic background, or socioeconomic status (see chapter 9). When there is such a genuine welcome, I suspect that there will be fewer ethnically homogeneous churches.

Does ethnic diversity, even language diversity, require denominational division? Language diversity is probably the most persuasive argument for such division, but I do not believe that speakers of different languages *must* be in separate denominations. It is possible to have, say, Korean-speaking presbyteries within a Presbyterian denomination, with the Korean-speaking churches sending English-speaking representatives to a combined General Assembly. It is awkward, but can we not remember that the early church was formed of Jew and Gentile (and of Jews from many nations and tongues)? They had all the problems we have and more, but they did not try to solve them by means of denominationalism. Acts 6:1–7 justifies additional programs in the church to promote fairness among different language and ethnic groups. Surely we have the resources to maintain that level of fairness within a united church today.

11

Dealing with Differences in Government

Differences in government fit under all the previous categories, but they pose particular problems for unity. One can consider toleration within many areas of doctrine and practice; but, after all, a single church, "the one, true church," can be governed only in one way. Or so it seems.

I don't have any easy answer here or in any other area of our discussion. It may be that in God's providence, governmental differences will prevent church union. Or perhaps that union will simply not be possible unless the Spirit, working contrary to the forces of denominationalism that tend to harden our differences, teaches the whole church some new things from the Scriptures.

Of course, ultimate reunion, by most prognostications, is a long way off, unless the Lord intends to come very soon. So, if we do not see an answer to the question of how the reorganized one, true church will be governed, for the present we can simply resolve to cross that bridge when we come to it, meanwhile chipping away at other barriers that may be easier to handle at the moment. It may be that in time we will be able to reorganize into three great evangelical denominations: one

108

episcopal, one presbyterian, and one congregational association. Once that is done we could start to worry about government! Meanwhile, let me say a few things about church government that may stimulate us to further thought.

The New Testament contains relatively little normative teaching about church government, compared to its teaching on the person of Christ, the atonement, the resurrection, the Spirit, justification, Christian morality, the last days. Much is said about the church as the body of Christ, about its gifts and unity, about its tasks in worship, evangelism, and instruction—but little is said about how it is to be governed. Although the Book of Acts makes clear that the apostles were the rulers of the church in their day and that they appointed assistants for various tasks (6:1ff), there is (remarkably) no indication of how the church is to be governed after the deaths of the apostles. The Pastoral Epistles and other books make references to church officers such as "bishops" and "elders"[1] and "deacons" and require obedience to them. Qualifications for these offices are stated (1 Tim. 3:1–13; Titus 1:5–9), and exhortations to the officers are made (Acts 20:17–37; 1 Peter 5:1–4), but their powers and relations to one another are never stated, and the manner of choosing them is somewhat obscure. In one case, something like an election seems to have taken place (Acts 6:3, 5); in another, an apostolic representative was given power to appoint (Titus 1:5). (The latter example may be taken to favor episcopacy, the former presbyterianism or congregationalism.)

I am, as I stated earlier, a "presbyterian," because I believe in a body of congregations connected to one another by a plurality of elected representative officers. I believe this because (1) I find in the New Testament some indication that the Christians followed in general the organization of the synagogues from which they came; because (2) it appears that bodies larger than local house-churches functioned as "churches"; and because (3) the New Testament always refers to church rulers ("the bishops," "the elders") in the plural. Pragmatically, the presbyterian form seems to me to allow the best combination of mutual accountability with local control and freedom, a system that forms the pattern, for example, for the remarkably successful structure of the United States civil government.

I would hope that the one, true church will one day, by God's grace, achieve reunion and adopt the presbyterian form of government as its pattern for reorganization. However, the arguments for presbyterianism summarized above are certainly not watertight; certainly they do not have the same force as those for the deity of Christ or salvation by grace. After all, the New Testament never *commands* us to follow the synagogue pattern alluded to above in (1). And, although the evidence for city-churches (presbyteries) is strong in the New Testament, it is harder to establish the existence of courts higher than those, except for that which included the apostolic band itself (Acts 15) and which had only one meeting that we know of; so (2) may not lead us to a full-blown presbyterian structure. Furthermore, although the New Testament speaks of bishops and elders in the plural (3), this fact does not quite prove that all churches were normatively required to have a plurality of elders. Can we be sure that there was never any church in which only one man was qualified for the eldership? Can we be sure that there were no distinctions of gifts, wisdom, and responsibilities among the elders such that one could become *primus inter pares?*

So, there is some uncertainty about the original form of government in the New Testament. If it were important to God that the church be governed only one way, I have no doubt that he would have made it more clear. Therefore, I am inclined to take the issue of church government a bit less seriously than many people do.[2] I think that God regards the structure and method of church government to be less important than the reality of Jesus' own government of the church as its supreme priest-king. The relative indifference of the New Testament to matters of human government would seem to be an invitation to us to take the reality of Jesus' own government more seriously. Related to this, perhaps another reason for the uncertainty about governmental structure is that this structure is less important than the spiritual qualities of the leaders and the people. When the proper spiritual qualities are lacking, even the best form of government (the presbyterian, in my view) will be a curse on God's people. When they are present, even inadequate forms of government will work well.[3]

Mutual trust is especially important. Many Christians (especially Presbyterians) think that no government will be adequate unless there are many checks and balances against the abuse of power, such as we find in the various denominational Forms of Government. But formal procedures become important only when there is conflict to be resolved or a distrust of informal agreements, and so on. Until Jesus returns, sin will be in the world, and we will always need some sorts of formal checks and balances, some formal procedures for doing things, some standard ways of redressing grievances. But the more mutual trust there is, the less of that will be necessary. The more we genuinely love each other, the less difference it will make whether, for example, there are three or five men on some committee or whether judicial appellants must first submit their appeals to a committee of presbytery.[4]

I suspect that if God ever permits the one, true church to reunite under a common government, he will at the same time bring about a great increase in our love and trust for one another. How else could reunion even be conceivable? When that happens, even though I dearly hope that the church will be presbyterian in structure, it won't bother me terribly if my dear brothers choose another system to govern God's people. I trust that this attitude of mine is not motivated by theological indifference, but by a desire to respect the emphasis and specific teaching of the Word of God, and to promote the unity of the church that the Word of God requires more clearly than it does any particular governmental structure.

Consider the following[5]:

We have seen that the relative silence in the New Testament about form of government is related to the importance of theocentric government, the rule of Christ himself through the Spirit. Bureaucracy and constitution are at best expressions of (the life of the Spirit) and of immense potential value because of it, at worst presiders over a corpse or a counterfeit.

Moreover, it could be argued that our fascination with bureaucracy and constitution is partly a cultural reflex of the attempt to map civic political power relations directly onto the church and vice versa. Thus the debates among congregationalists, presbyterians, and episcopalians recapitulate the debates among democrats, republicans, monarchists.

Granting, then, that the fundamental issue for the New Testament is the rule of God through the Spirit, the biblical method of determining policy must be not majority vote as such, but Spirit-generated consensus among the leadership. The elders did have Christ's authority to rule, but they recognized a world of difference between godly rule and worldly tyranny. They were to rule in a unique, nonworldly way, as "servant-leaders," following the steps of Jesus himself (Matt. 20:26–28). Further, they knew that they were not the depositories of all wisdom, and no leader with any sense thinks that he can drive the sheep where they have no inkling to go. Good leadership is always consultative, in the sense of consulting the well-being of those led. It listens to the whole people of God, and particularly to those for whom it is responsible. Of course it does not merely capitulate to what the sheep already think their well-being is, but educates them. And by educating them it is able to lead them rather than simply driving them.

But that means that in a healthy church the debate between congregationalism and presbyterianism is largely an academic one. What difference does it make to spiritual life? If you start with the leaders (presbyterianism), you nevertheless discover at the heart of biblical leadership the consultative, or, better, servant pattern, which recognizes and uses the gifts (including gifts of administration) residing in the congregation as a whole and in its members individually in varying degrees. If you start with the congregation (congregationalism), you find at the heart of biblical wisdom in the congregation's decision-making the necessary conviction that some are more gifted and that their gifts (which are gifts of the Lord and not merely the congregation's property to manage as it wishes) must be given full scope for exercise.

The *differences* between the two emerge when controversy strikes. There the formal constitution determines the rules of the fight. In such cases, however, congregationalism can degenerate into mob mania and presbyterianism into high-handedness. Then the only solution is to recover the spiritual priority: Spirit-led consensus, servant leadership. While broader courts can help some (and thus I prefer presbyterianism), our goal is not to have some solution imposed by a broader authority, but to have restored the brotherly unity of mind that comes only from God's grace.

Now let us perspectivalize episcopacy. James is the informal bishop in Acts 15, I think. Any good bishop acts like any other good leader—he is consultative. James sums up the arguments, the state of consensus. By doing so he may even create somewhat greater consensus. But how could anyone with the biblical wisdom necessary to become a bishop think that all wisdom was summed up in him or in his superiors alone? He has listened to a debate and almost certainly learned something from it. Outside of modern constitutional arrangements, many traditional cultures operate a good deal by consensus. There are, of course, the usual opportunities for abuse. But again wise leaders can't get too far ahead of their followers. And wise minorities will know when to show proper deference to leaders, even when the consensus of those leaders is distasteful to them.

On the above principles, a monarchical bishop would not be a terribly bad thing, especially if (1) he were appointed from below, by consensus, rather than from above (though it would be proper for the consensus to be influenced by those who are already in leadership positions), and (2) one can make an appeal over the bishop to correct abuses. One thinks of the checks and balances in the United States Constitution; analogous checks could help in the church situation.

What of independency? The independents have given up on all constitutions and bureaucracies broader than the parish size (what an arbitrary stopping point!) mostly because they see people preoccupied

with the formal structures and not with the spiritual life that the structures are supposed to facilitate.

The main conclusion: If we take seriously the biblical principles—(1)
that God himself rules the church, (2) through his Word by way of
Spirit-led consensus, (3) administered by servant leaders who understand their limitations and the gifts of others in the body—then the
practical differences between presbyterianism, congregationalism, and
episcopacy would be very small. These terms, indeed, could describe a
single form of government from three different perspectives!

The way to unity is precisely a renewal of that love and respect for
God and one another that will lead to a Spirit-led church government.[6] As I write these words, incredible changes in government are
occurring in what once was "the Communist bloc." Can we not pray
that God will work within his own people as well, to bring about the
kinds of government that will honor him and therefore lead to
reunion?

Notes

1. As do most Presbyterians, I believe that the words *bishop* and *elder* are synonymous, the
latter term being more easily understood among Jews and the former among Gentiles.

2. No one, at least, claims that one particular form of government is essential to the existence
of the true church, so that any body without that form of government is not really a church.
Most would therefore agree that their particular system of church government is part of the
"well being" *(bene esse)* not the "being" *(esse)* of the church.

3. Someone might ask: "If church government is relatively unimportant, then why the blis-
tering attack on denominational separation? Isn't that essentially a question about church government?" My reply: (1) One may make a plausible biblical case for either episcopalian, presbyterian, or congregational government; but there is *no* case to be made for denominationalism. And
(2) the issue of denominationalism is not only an issue of church government, but also concerns
fellowship, mutual sharing of gifts, our full expression of brotherly love, the church's theological
unity, our witness to the world, and many other matters. If the issue were only one of singular vs.
multiple or centralized vs. diversified government, I would not be sufficiently interested to write
a book about it.

4. These are the sorts of questions that are debated endlessly, it seems, at presbytery meetings
and spelled out meticulously in the various books of church government and canon law.

5. The next eight paragraphs are my paraphrases of a letter sent to me by Vern Poythress. I
thought the letter was a vintage example of the "multi-perspectivalism" that he and I both
emphasize. Some of the following words are his own, but I will not use quotation marks, for I
intend, as I must, to take responsibility for any problems emerging from my formulation.

6. Besides the letter from Poythress, I was greatly moved by a recent interview in which
Rousas J. Rushdoony describes the government of his denomination, the "Anglican Churches of
America and Associates." His emphasis also is that government should be first pastoral and consultative and that this emphasis should far outweigh the bureaucratic and judicial elements. I had
never heard of this denomination before, but from Rushdoony's description it is enormously
attractive to me. (See Susan Alder, "Background: An Interview with R. J. Rushdoony on Church
Government," *Christian Observer,* 3 November 1989, pp. 17–18.)

12

● ●

Dealing with Differences in Priorities

Rarely mentioned among the sources of denominational division are what I would call differences in "priorities," or "emphasis." These are not differences in doctrine, for two bodies may adhere to the same doctrines but have very different priorities. We might describe them as practical or historical differences, but they are distinct enough even within those classifications to deserve special mention. One major problem in the quest for reunion, I think, is the tendency to confuse priority questions with other sorts of doctrinal and practical questions.

Perhaps the best way to understand this issue is first to look at the nature of priorities in the individual Christian life and then, by comparison, at the nature of priorities within denominations.

Priorities among Ultimates

When God says *no* to us, he requires an immediate response. When he says "do not steal," and I am stealing, I must stop immediately. I have no right to ask him to wait. Repentance, turning from sin, is not a long, drawn-out process, but a single act.[1]

But when God says *yes,* the situation is not quite that clear-cut. His positive commands require a somewhat different sort of response from his negative commands. On the positive side, God commands us to pray, evangelize, worship, feed the hungry, visit the sick, study the Scriptures, train our children, edify fellow believers, seek justice in society, show love to our spouses, even replenish and subdue the earth, and so on. Does he expect instant, immediate obedience to those commands?

We may be inclined to say yes, and that inclination comes from a good motive. We think of Abraham, who heard the word of God to leave Ur of the Chaldees and simply got up and did it. Even more impressive is his seemingly instantaneous obedience to the awful divine command to sacrifice Isaac, his beloved son and the heir of the promise.[2] We think of the disciples, who stopped whatever they were doing and obeyed Jesus' command to follow him. We think of Jesus himself, who readily obeyed the Father's every wish. There seems to be here a pattern of immediate, instantaneous obedience as a model for our own.

Surely there are times when God calls us to do something *now.* Jesus did not accept would-be disciples who wanted first to say good-bye to others or to bury their dead. He wanted them right away. But God does not always command us to do something "now." Indeed, God commands us to do many things that can *not* all be done immediately. Think of every positive thing God commands (some of them listed in the fourth paragraph of this chapter). So many things we must do! In the nature of the case, they simply cannot be done "now." If I spend the morning going door to door, presenting the gospel to people in my neighborhood, I won't be able to visit my sick friend in the hospital until afternoon. If I spend the next hour in prayer, I shall have to postpone writing this chapter of my book, and so on.

So I come to an obvious yet somehow surprising conclusion: that some good works must be *postponed.* Obeying God is not always a simple matter of hearing his command, then going out and doing it immediately. Sometimes we must put off a good work until tomorrow so that we may do another today. Sometimes when I hear God speaking in the Scriptures, I must reply, "Lord, I'll do that later; you have given me something else to do now."

This means that in relation to God's commands, each of us must develop a system of *priorities.* We must discover not only what God requires, but also which command to carry out first. Priorities among ultimates! Priorities among absolutes! The whole idea sounds so paradoxical. We are not used to thinking along these lines. We normally assume that if two commands are absolute, that is, from God, neither can take precedence over the other. But we know now that this cannot be correct.

The problem faces us every day, even every moment. What shall I do *first*? What shall I do *now*? Generally we make our decisions without really thinking much about priorities. We make priority decisions off the tops of our heads, unreflectively. Yet these choices often have enormous consequences. Where can we turn for help?

On the problem of priorities among ultimates, sermons often do more harm than good. Sermons almost never tell us which good works we may leave until later! They never tell us which prayers may be left unsaid (for now), which Scriptures unread, which needy people unfed, unvisited, unevangelized, uninstructed. In fact, it would be hard to imagine a sermon that did tell us such things. The very nature of the sermon seems to be that of encouraging us to *do*, not to leave undone.

There are good reasons why sermons are like that, though I will not list them here. What is harder to justify, however, is that sermons often not only fail to solve our priority questions, but they often also make those questions more difficult.[3] For sermons usually imply, if they do not actually suggest, that we should be doing *all* good works *all* the time.

One week we are told that evangelism is absolutely central to the work of the church and the life of the believer. Everyone must be passionately concerned about evangelism. And if we are passionately concerned, of course, we will spend time evangelizing. The preacher may present to us as illustration a Christian who has led thirty people into the kingdom during the past year. Such illustrations make us ashamed of ourselves.

Next week the sermon is on prayer. We are told that our lives must be full of prayer. If we don't spend a lot of time praying, we don't really love God and our neighbors. And Luther spent so much time praying each day! Again we are ashamed. Then the next week we hear about feeding the hungry, then studying the Bible, then contending against false doctrines, then influencing our social institutions, then working hard at our jobs, then caring for our families. And of course we must not "forsake the assembly," which seems to mean attending every church meeting possible.

I am a church musician, and I once preached a sermon that showed by a good biblico-theological method the centrality of *music* in the Christian life. We are, after all, saved to sing the praises of Christ (1 Peter 2:9). Since all of us ought to put much more time than we do into our worship life, we ought to study how to worship, just as we study how to pray and how to witness. And if we really care, we'll join the choir!

But when we count up all the things we are supposed to do, we have to ask hard questions about them. Is it really right for preachers to heap such an enormous sense of shame on their people? Though all these things are "central,"[4] "vital," "important," though all of them deserve a passionate concern and a sacrificial giving of time and resources, we cannot do them all at once. Ought we to be ashamed of that? Why, even if we tried to do all these things at once, the end result would be a lot of failure, frustration—and shame!

That is one side of the problem. The opposite result is also possible: that failure to come to grips with this issue can lead to pride and arrogance. Believers are often very suspicious of other believers who have a different set of priorities from their own. The zealous evangelist who labors many hours to bring the gospel to neighbors and friends may look down at his stay-at-home brother who spends more time with his wife and children—and vice versa.

How do we deal with the problem? First, let us recognize that God understands our finitude. He does not expect us to do everything at once. He commanded Adam and Eve to "fill the earth and subdue it" (Gen. 1:28), but he did not intend for them to do that immediately or all by themselves. For at the same time as he told them to subdue the earth, he also told them to "be fruitful" and replenish it: he ordained reproduction. Subduing the earth was not a job for Adam and Eve alone, but for a great body of men, women, and children spread over the whole surface of the globe. Similarly, when Jesus called the disciples to teach all nations (Matt. 28:19f), he did not intend for the twelve disciples to do the whole job themselves and instantly. He envisaged, rather, a historical process (a long one, as it has turned out) with millions of believers cooperating in this great task. Not all believers do the same thing, either. They have different gifts (1 Cor. 12; Rom. 12) and therefore different callings, but each one makes a contribution. Some will knock on doors, some will develop businesses to support those knocking on doors,[5] some will pray for those who are knocking on doors, and so on.

And, when God calls me to pray, as he does in Scripture, he does not necessarily mean that I should drop everything and do it immediately and for an unlimited time. Even Jesus got up from his prayers to do other things. Rather, God expects me to devote a reasonable amount of time to prayer. How much is "reasonable" depends on the person. Some have more opportunity and leisure for this than others (like the "order of widows" in the New Testament [1 Tim. 5:3–16, esp. v. 5]). Gifts and calling make a difference. How do we determine our gifts and calling? General principles of Scripture, our opportunities and abilities, the support of the church (cf. Acts 13:2, etc.), the Holy Spirit enabling us to make our decisions according to love (Phil. 1:9f; cf. Rom. 12:1f; Eph. 5:8–10).

Some, then, are called to pray more than others, some to knock on more doors, and so on. Those with one gift/calling are not to look down on those who have another, for they are one body in Christ. One is like the hand, another like the foot, another like the brain. Each needs the others if the body is to function correctly (1 Cor. 12). No one should feel guilty,[6] and no one should develop arrogant pride.

Denominational Priorities

Now we can say things about denominations similar to what we have been saying about individual Christians. Among the many kinds of differences they have, the priorities of denominations also differ from one another. One may give special attention to Christian education, another to evangelism, another to social action. One will have a strong interest in maintaining proper procedures; another will at times cut corners in the established procedures to accomplish some other goal. The point is not that Denomination A believes in, say, Christian education while Denomination B does not. (What denomination would dare say that they don't believe in teaching the gospel to their children?) Rather, some denominations put a higher emphasis, or priority, on Christian education than do others.

The same applies to more doctrinal matters. Say that Denomination A emphasizes that God is to be worshiped "with reverence and awe" (Heb. 12:28); Denomination B emphasizes that worship must be of such a style that demonstrates God's love to the people who attend (James 2:1–13). Denomination B certainly would not wish to deny Hebrews 12:28, nor would Denomination A wish to deny James 2:1–13. But there is a difference of emphasis/priority between them that can lead, indeed, to rather different styles of worship.

Other differences are partly due to differing priorities, partly to simple disagreements. I certainly would not reduce the difference between Calvinism and Arminianism to a difference in priority or emphasis.[7] These are differences of exegesis, of theology. But there is an *element* of priority difference here, too. For when a Calvinist tests his doctrinal formulations, he tends to be preoccupied with the impact of that formulation on the divine sovereignty, though he also wishes to do justice to human responsibility. Arminians, however, while not wishing to deny the sovereignty of God, tend to be more preoccupied with the need for a credible doctrine of human responsibility. It is interesting to speculate as to which came first, the priority difference or the substantive difference. (I am inclined to say the former, in most cases.) Perhaps if both parties had tried harder to appreciate the priorities of each other, their difference might not have hardened into a substantive one. And perhaps the only way out will be for both parties to develop their arguments with a greater appreciation for where the other party is coming from. For neither *priority* is wrong, in my view.[8] Since neither is wrong, there is room for mutual encouragement and affirmation at the priority level, an affirmation that ought to precede and govern all debate.

In my view, priority differences alone should not separate denominations. Consider the Orthodox Presbyterian Church (OPC) and the Presbyterian Church in America (PCA), two bodies with which I have had some experience and which have considered church union (unsuccessfully) from time to time. These two denominations have identical doctrinal standards, and both have shown a serious purpose in maintaining those doctrinal commitments. There is a somewhat wider range of opinion in the PCA on some matters: the precise scope of Christian liberty, for instance. But those differences are very slight. Yet there is a kind of nervousness in both groups about the possibility of church union. Why? Well, for one thing, there are in both groups many misunderstandings about the role of denominations in God's kingdom, misunderstandings that I hope this book will help to alleviate.[9] But, for another thing, there are definite differences in priorities between the two bodies, differences that provoke a sense of discomfort in those contemplating merger.

The PCA has a far larger missions program for its size than the OPC, though both bodies certainly believe in missions and support it.[10] The OPC gives much more support, per capita, to the production of Christian-education materials. The OPC is known for its profound and brilliant theologians, the PCA for its remarkable church growth. The OPC is known for the carefulness with which it follows presbyterian procedures, the PCA for its speed (sometimes at the expense of "procedures") in getting new churches started.[11] Some have described the OPC as more inward-facing and the PCA as more outward-facing, to recall a previous distinction. The OPC is known for its relatively tough ordination exams, the PCA for its openness in welcoming new ministers and churches into the body.

A bit of whimsy may clarify the issue. The OPC is like a homemaker, the PCA like a breadwinner. In the traditional family (rapidly disappearing, one would gather from the national media), the husband is the breadwinner, the wife the homemaker. The homemaker spends more time at home. She sees that the house is clean, that the children are taught the right things, that the right persons are on the guest list and the wrong ones excluded. The breadwinner, on the other hand, concentrates his energies outside the home. He knows the house has to be kept in order, and he is glad that there is somebody around to do that work. But his own talents and interests lead him to take on more and more responsibilities on behalf of those outside the household. He knows he must meet *their* needs, not only those of his family; and he knows that if he does not go into the world to draw from the world's supply of wealth, his family will not survive. Homemaker and breadwinner may well respect each other's priorities, or they may fight about them. At least it should be noted that their priorities are not the same.

Many in the OPC and in the PCA now believe that their differences in priority are incompatible. They think that the two churches cannot join together unless they become more like one another. I think that these opponents of union fail to see the distinction between doctrinal differences and priority differences—or they fail to understand that the differences between the two groups are indeed largely differences in priority. If I am right that the differences involve priorities, the two groups ought not to remain apart. For the two kinds of gifts are complementary, not in opposition. The PCA needs more theologians and Christian educators; the OPC needs more evangelists and church planters. Each needs the help of the other in deciding when and how much to bend "procedures" to hasten the advance of the gospel. Or, to revert to my metaphor, the homemaker needs a breadwinner, and vice versa. When we recognize that homemaker-gifts and breadwinner-gifts are complementary, our sense of the possibilities can change. After all, homemakers often fall in love with and marry breadwinners, and these sometimes live (relatively) "happily ever after."

What is it that enables us to see differences as they really are, without exaggerating them? The love of Christ. Love and marriage go together, in the spiritual world as in the natural world; and it is love that holds the marriage together.

As we seek to evaluate our relationships to other denominations, we will observe many sorts of differences. But it is important for us to distinguish substantive differences from priority differences, even when sometimes (as in the Calvinist/Arminian example) these types of differences are both found together. Making that distinction will give us a much clearer view of things and will also, I believe, naturally pressure us toward reunion. As we saw earlier, denominationalism is largely responsible for the present uneven distribution of gifts in the church and for the inaccessibility of the gifts of some to Christians of other denominations. A determination to redress this imbalance will force us to work toward reunion.

Emphasis in Ministry

Love will also enable us to make wiser judgments about what to *emphasize* in the preaching and teaching of our churches. This is an important "priority" question that all of us have to face. In my previous book[12] I attacked the tendency for theologians to criticize one another on the basis of emphasis: "Theologian A does not sufficiently emphasize X." I pointed out there that there is room for many differences in emphasis, since the work of theology is to apply biblical content, not merely to state it. Even relatively minor matters, like the head coverings of women in 1 Corinthians 11, are proper subject matter for theology, even if the theologian does not attempt in the same context to emphasize more central biblical topics.

In this regard, however, pastors are different from other theologians. Most people get 90 percent or so of their Christian teaching from a local church. It is therefore important that the ministry of that local church provide a balanced diet of spiritual nourishment. An academic theologian can sometimes afford to spend his life studying obscure subjects of interest to him but not to many others in the church. But the pastor of a church cannot afford that kind of luxury. If the teaching ministry of a church "majors in minors" or "rides hobby horses," the people will not be fed.

The proper emphasis of church ministry must be, roughly, the emphasis of Scripture itself. I say "roughly," because the Word must be applied to the people in the congregation, and of course these people are very different from the people to whom the New Testament was first addressed. We must talk about many things today that Paul did not talk about: abortion, nuclear war, Christian influence in politics, television violence, pornography, and so on. Still, the center of our preaching and teaching (and indeed the "answer," in a sense, even to the modern problems) must always be "Jesus Christ and him crucified" (1 Cor. 2:2). This is the great message that all true Christian churches share, regardless of denomination.

One anti-ecumenical tendency is for churches to emphasize their *distinctives,* the doctrines and practices that separate them from other churches, denominations, and traditions, at the expense of those doctrines and practices held more broadly, by all evangelicals or even by all Christians. Some churches, for example, that believe the premillennial view of Christ's return put such an emphasis on it, even making it a test of orthodoxy, as to produce an imbalance in their teaching and an unnecessary degree of separation from other believers. Whether or not that doctrine is true is not the point right now. The question is whether that should be a major emphasis of the church's preaching and teaching, coordinate with, say, the resurrection of Jesus.

I believe that we should accept a wide variety of different emphases in different ministries. Again, no one can do everything, and so no one can have a perfect balance. At the same time, some emphases are better than others, and we ought in general to emphasize the more important matters over those that are less important. For the most part, the "more important" matters, as scripturally determined, coincide with those doctrines and practices believed broadly throughout the Christian church, rather than the distinctives of any one denomination. Such emphasis will be beneficial to church unity, but also to the very quality of ministry within the church. Fewer lessons are needed as much as the lesson to put first things first.

Denominational chauvinism often includes the view that the distinctives of one's denomination are more important than the great doctrines shared among all Christians. This attitude often leads to serious imbalances in preaching and teaching. On the contrary, I would maintain that denominational distinctives *never* have that kind of importance (more on this in chapter 14).

Notes

1. I recently heard of a man being disciplined by his church for adultery who said that he was "in the process of repenting." What he meant was that he was committing adultery less frequently than before! That is not biblical repentance.

2. To be sure, we should not assume that the Genesis account tells us everything that happened. It may well be, for example, that Abraham wrestled with the divine command before he left Ur. But Romans 4:20–21 commend Abraham on the whole as one who did not "waver" in his obedience to God's words.

3. In case anyone is curious, my pastor, Dick Kaufmann, is not guilty of any of the following criticisms of preachers. If anything, I am mainly criticizing my own preaching.

4. One interesting thing about Christianity is the great many things in it that can be called central. It is a circle with many centers; or perhaps only *one* (Christ), which can be seen from many points of view—"perspectival."

5. I am not, incidentally, saying that this is the only justification for working in a business. The cultural mandate of Genesis 1:28 is also an important basis for it.

6. Unless, of course, he neglects his calling.

7. A *priority* often coincides with what in an earlier chapter I called a *perspective*.

8. As I argued in my *Doctrine of the Knowledge of God* (Phillipsburg, N.J.: Presbyterian and Reformed, 1987), it is legitimate and illuminating to read Scripture from a great many "perspectives" and emphases. See also Vern Poythress, *Symphonic Theology* (Grand Rapids: Zondervan, 1987).

9. If I may venture a slightly exaggerated summary, which would probably be disputed in both bodies: the OPC believes in church unity, but only with a perfect partner; the PCA does not believe very deeply in church unity at all. At least that's the way it looks to me.

10. The PCA has the fastest-growing foreign missions force in the world. The OPC recently had to cut back its foreign-missions program because of financial constraints.

11. When I was in the OPC, its presbyteries seemed to spend forever perfecting their minutes. I often wished someone had asked seriously how high a priority God would have us place on the perfection of minutes! Most presbyters, I'm sure, did not think of it as a priority matter at all, but as obedience to a divine command that "everything should be done in a fitting and orderly way" (1 Cor. 14:40). But, like all divine commands, this one needs to be placed in an order of priority in comparison with other such commands. The danger is that we try to keep Command A perfectly (perhaps for the trivial reason that it is first on a presbytery's docket) and never get to command B.

12. J. Frame, *Doctrine of the Knowledge of God*, pp. 182–183.

13

* *

Dealing with
Our Attitudes

At the root of the whole problem of church division lies our own cussedness, our sinful attitudes. We saw earlier that denominationalism encourages such frames of mind, but of course it is a chicken-and-egg situation. Wrong attitudes cause division, and they are also fed by it.

Embracing all other sinful attitudes is *lack of love,* love for God and for one another (Matt. 22:37–40). Our lack of love for God keeps us from hearing his Word and from being willing to make radical changes in our values and practices. We would rather keep the fleeting benefits of denominationalism than claim by faith the far greater blessings that come from doing things God's way.

The Symptoms

Our lack of love for one another, which derives from lovelessness toward God, manifests itself in a number of ways:[1]

1. *Pride, boastfulness, arrogance* (Ps. 10:2; 59:12; 73:6; Prov. 8:13; 11:2; 13:10; 14:3; 16:18; 29:23; Isa. 23:9; 25:11; Jer. 48:29; 49:16; Mark 7:22; 1 Tim. 3:6; 6:4; 1 John 2:6). We tend to look on what God has done in our denominational fellowships as if it were our own

achievement and the unique property of our own group. Somehow these accomplishments seem to reflect better on ourselves when there are fewer people to share them with. Conversely, just as it is difficult to admit our own errors and faults, it is very difficult for us to admit such errors and faults in our denominations.

2. *Contentiousness, discord, strife* (Prov. 13:10a; 18:6; 19:13; 21:19; 22:10; 27:15; Hab. 1:3; Rom. 2:8; 1 Cor. 1:11; 11:16; Phil. 1:15–17; 1 Tim. 6:4; Titus 3:9f). "Pride only breeds quarrels," says the first passage in Proverbs from our group of references. Because we want glory for ourselves, we seek to find fault in others. Contentious people are constantly looking for something to argue about, some way to start controversy and disrupt the peace.

Contentiousness can be difficult to identify, for one man's contentiousness is another man's "zeal for the truth." Zeal for the truth is certainly a virtue. But one's energetic efforts deserve that title only when they are grounded in a realistic biblical understanding of what the truth really is, including Scripture's teachings about unity and about priorities. A constant insistence that we achieve perfection in some one area of church life before doing anything else is not a proper zeal for the truth; rather, it is contentiousness. Dwelling on the faults of other denominations out of proportion to their importance is contentiousness.

Contentious people believe the worst about others, frequently taking the statements of others in the worst possible sense, rather than giving others the benefit of the doubt ("innocent until proven guilty"). Surely that has had much to do with the animosities underlying the church's divisions.

Contentiousness is related to oversensitivity; when someone says an even slightly critical word about a contentious person, the latter will rush to defend himself. He cannot abide the idea of being wrong or of being thought wrong by others. Yet there is little consideration for the feelings of those whom he wishes to criticize. Although he considers himself free to interpret their words and deeds in the worst possible sense, others are supposed to make all sorts of allowances and excuses for his excesses. Of such people it is often said, "He can dish it out, but he can't take it." Such a person will often have a double standard when evaluating denominations: one standard for his own, another for the others. He will tend to defend his denomination as he defends himself—while, without justification, finding all sorts of fault with those outside.

It can be difficult to identify contentiousness in others, at least to identify it well enough to make them accountable to formal discipline. But I am confident that Christians can usually recognize it in themselves if they call on the indwelling Spirit to open their eyes. The trouble is that our pride often keeps us from even considering that we might be guilty of such a seriously sinful attitude. Let us hear what the above Scriptures have to say to us, as well as the following, which urge positively a gentle and peaceful attitude: 2 Samuel 20:19; Zechariah 8:19; Matthew 5:9; Galatians 6:1; James 3:17; 5:19; 1 Peter 3:11.

3. *Envy, jealousy* (Exod. 20:17; Prov. 23:17; 27:4; Matt. 27:18; Acts 13:45; 17:5; Rom. 1:29; Phil. 1:15; 1 Tim. 6:4). Envy is not just a desire to take unjustly what belongs to others, but it is also what Nietzsche called *ressentiment*, or hatred of others for their accomplishments and success. It is the reverse side of pride. We wish to glorify ourselves, so we hate those achievements that allow others to glorify themselves, perhaps at our expense. Thus, churches that are strong in teaching but weak in evangelism will often feel constrained to find some fault in those to whom God has given some evangelistic success. The reverse is also true, though in my experience to a lesser degree.

4. *Harshness*, the opposite of gentleness (Isa. 40:11; 2 Cor. 10:1; Gal. 5:22; 1 Thess. 2:7; 2 Tim. 2:24; Titus 3:2; James 3:17; 1 Peter 2:18). Harshness exaggerates the faults and errors of others, both as to the degree of evil and as to the measures we should take against it.

5. *Xenophobia, snobbery*, rather than welcoming hospitality to other Christians (Rom. 12:13; 1 Tim. 3:2; Titus 1:8; 1 Peter 4:9). Frankly, we all have a great desire to stay with what is familiar, with our own people, our own ways of doing things. We don't want to have to deal with other ethnic or socioeconomic groups in the fellowship of our churches. We don't want to have to deal with the priority concerns of those in other theological traditions. We don't want to have to endure challenges from them or to be answerable to them.

6. *Party spirit* (1 Cor. 1–3). The partisan mentality ignores our responsibility to love all in the body. It prefers to give allegiance only to its own particular faction, which may be united by respect for a particular leader or leadership style or by preference for some doctrinal or practical emphasis.

7. *Superficiality, immaturity* (1 Cor. 2:6; 14:20; 2 Cor. 13:11; Eph. 4:13f; Phil. 3:12; Col. 1:28; 3:16; 4:12; 2 Tim. 3:16, 17; Heb. 12:23; 13:21; 1 Peter 5:10). We need to grow in our understanding of what God's Word says about these issues, willing to be taught and not taking for granted what we have heard in the past.

8. *Anger, wrath, bitterness, vengeance* (Deut. 32:35; Ps. 94:1; Matt.

5:22; Rom. 12:19; Gal. 5:20; Eph. 4:26, 31; Col. 3:8, 21; Titus 1:7; James 1:19f). There is godly anger, like the zeal of Christ for the holiness of God's temple. But Scripture usually presents human anger as a sinful or even murderous lack of love. Anger seeks to replace God's vengeance with our own. It holds grudges, refusing to forgive (Matt. 18:21). There is much of this, I believe, in the movement to perpetuate division in the church. God says in his Word that anger should be dealt with *quickly*. "Do not let the sun go down while you are still angry" (Eph. 4:26; cf. Matt. 5:23–26; 18:15–20). Reconciliation is a high priority in God's kingdom. Instead, the nature of unrighteous anger is to indulge itself, to put off reconciliation, to harbor a grudge.

9. *Ambition, avarice* (Titus 1:7; 2 Peter 2:10). Those who are interested in personal power or advancement often reinforce denominational divisions. It is easier to achieve prominence (by worldly means) in a small group than in a large one, easier in a human denomination than in God's trans-denominational church. Rather than risk the end of their prominence in the uncertainty inherent in church merger, influential denominational bureaucrat types often stand in the way of biblical reunion. This is a large part of the problem; for these are the types of people most often appointed to ecumenism committees, the ones who most often must be satisfied with any negotiation.

10. *Lack of openness, honesty* (John 15:15). Too often when representatives of different denominations hold discussions, there is a reticence, an unwillingness to share what it is that *really* stands in the way of union. We need to remember again that in such cases we are dealing with other Christian brothers and sisters, with whom we can share family secrets without embarrassment.

Revival and Reunion

In all of the above and other ways we sin against God and against others and thereby violate the law of love. To put it differently, we create adversary relationships between ourselves and other believers, seeing them as enemies to be conquered, rather than as brothers and sisters to be cherished.

How good it is to know that, unlike angry and contentious human beings, our God is a God of love and forgiveness: "If we confess our sins, he is faithful and just and will forgive us our sins and purify us from all unrighteousness" (1 John 1:9). May this gracious God move us to confess and receive forgiveness, the forgiveness bought with the blood of his only Son.

Students of revival have often said that revival begins with taking sin more seriously, with people truly mourning over the blackness of their guilt before God. While I do not believe God authorizes us to go through periods of black despair without a sense of grace, it is certainly true that we will not appreciate the greatness of our salvation until we have seen how much our sins have offended God, how truly wretched those sins are in his sight.

And I rather think that reunion will not come without revival. Revival does tend to break down denominational barriers between Christians, though often in the end those who break free from the old denominations wind up in a new one! Perhaps true reunion will depend on a revival that does not die, that does not fossilize itself into a new denominational program.

At any rate, Jesus' concern for unity demands that we all take a good look at ourselves, a look that will have beneficial effects in all areas of the church's ministry.

In this chapter I have been rather negative, focusing on the bad attitudes that we should avoid. To balance it, I have included as an Appendix a very positive treatment, a beautiful little sermon on "Peacemakers" by my colleague Dennis E. Johnson. Please take time to read it.

Notes

1. Compare T. M'Crie's treatment of this issue in *The Unity of the Church* (Dallas, Tex.: Presbyterian Heritage Publications, 1989), pp. 33ff, 118ff. The former passage deals with attitudes that work against church unity, the latter those attitudes most conducive to unity.

14

● ●

Dealing with
Our Assumptions

Besides the attitudes of our hearts, we must also become more self-conscious about the assumptions or presuppositions we bring to the question of church union. Some of these assumptions may be unconscious, in the sense that we do not explicitly *say* them, also in the sense that we do not reflect on them. Yet they do influence our decisions, our attitudes, our openness or lack of openness to the views of others. They even influence the way we *see* reality, for assumptions do influence observations.[1] Very often we see what we want to see. The mind is selective. It screens out data that is unsuited to our preconceptions, and it evaluates that data in the light of its established value system.

In my experience, attempts at church union have often been frustrated by assumptions such as those on the following list. They are all, in my estimation, untrue and unbiblical. So we may profitably ask ourselves whether any of these assumptions are lurking in our own hearts.

1. *"Nothing much of religious significance can be learned from outside of my own [denominational or theological] tradition."* But I ask: Is it likely that God has limited spiritual wisdom to some small segment

of his body—a segment, moreover, that exists as the result of sin? God's wisdom is given to his whole body, though to be sure there are some imbalances among gifts within individual denominations, as we have seen.

I continue to believe that the Reformed theological tradition is superior to all others as a general rule. Yet I am constantly impressed with the wisdom that God has given to people of other backgrounds. They say things that are unquestionably biblical, but that would never have been put that way by a Reformed teacher. For example, I am coming to love Gregorian chants, much to my surprise.

2. *"The distinctives of my tradition are more important than the doctrines and practices that we share with other traditions."* Few would admit to holding this assumption. Still, I think many Christians feel this way; for the things that really excite them about the Christian faith are the distinctives of one tradition rather than the common property of the universal church. Such people are understandably reluctant to consider merging with other bodies and perhaps losing those distinctives. But can anyone seriously maintain such a view? Is the Lutheran view of Christ's ubiquity more important than the universal church conviction as to the deity of Christ? Is the charismatic experience of being "slain in the spirit" more important than justification by faith?

My own view is that the most important things are the things that are most broadly confessed across denominational and theological traditions. I value the Reformed distinctives chiefly because they give me a coherent theological account of those trans-denominational truths. It is the Reformed faith, in my view, that gives the most consistent *account* of the reality and sovereignty of God, the Creator-creature distinction (Chalcedon), the doctrine of the Trinity, the death and resurrection of Christ for us. I would encourage my Methodist, Baptist, Episcopal, and other Christian brothers and sisters to value their traditions for similar reasons, if they can do that.

3. *"The distinctives of my tradition must be preserved at all costs in any church union."* To say this is to deny the point made earlier, that Scripture warrants and necessitates a certain amount of theological tolerance.

4. *"Since the truth is at stake, we cannot enter any union until we are convinced that no erroneous teaching will be permitted."* Same reply here. There will never be a perfect church, and no constitution or negotiation can guarantee inerrant preaching and teaching. The issue is the *extent* to which tolerance of different views will be permitted.

5. *"We should not merge with any church that uses extrabiblical data in its determination of policy."* There is truth here: Scripture alone is our ultimate standard *(sola scriptura)*. But Scripture must be applied to circumstances, and to do that we must understand both the Scriptures and the circumstances. To deny that is to betray a false (unbiblical) concept of scriptural sufficiency. Although the issue of scriptural sufficiency is important, that principle must be stated precisely, not according to someone's vague feeling about what it means.

6. *"We should not unite with any body that does not share our empha-sis on [this or that]."* This is an even worse misunderstanding than 1 through 4 above, and my replies to those apply to this one also. God's word expresses a wide variety of different "emphases." The teaching ministry of the church, as I indicated earlier, should focus on the *central* message of Scripture, which is shared among all the churches. Beyond that, Scripture warrants considerable flexibility, as we apply its text to the ever-changing situations of our day. (See my earlier discussion of "priorities.")

7. *"In a union, nothing should be agreed simply on the basis of trust."* This implies that all the details of our future church life must be stated in writing, formally, with consequences of violation clearly spelled out. But churches will never unite if they insist on formally spelling out *all* the details of their life together. Indeed, the more biblical procedure is to merge first, *then* to work out differences! (See chapter 16.) As in a marriage, trust is all-important. If there is no basic trust, no formal procedures will insure the permanence of union. But if there is substantial trust, formal statements and procedures (which are *not* emphasized in Scripture) are relatively unimportant.

Notes

1. See Thomas Kuhn, *The Structure of Scientific Revolutions* (Chicago: Univ. of Chicago Press, 1962, 1970). On the application of "presuppositionalism" to theology, see Cornelius Van Til, *The Defense of the Faith* (Phillipsburg, N.J.: Presbyterian and Reformed, 1975).

15

* * * * * * * * * * * * * * * * * * *

Evaluating Churches

If God is pleased to bring about reunion of his one, true church, I tend to think that it will be a step-by-step process. Most likely, denominations will first merge with those denominations that are most like themselves. Then those larger, more diverse denominations will merge with others most like themselves and so on, doubtless with many roadblocks along the way. One alternative might be an "evangelical COCU":[1] a possibly large group of denominations, perhaps including some with major differences between them, covenanting to pray, study, and work together, however long it may take to bring about a large-scale reunion. Obviously, various modifications and combinations of these ideas are possible. Others are certainly more likely than I to hit on the right strategy. Those so gifted should definitely begin thinking up a good plan.

If we are to be prepared to take steps in any such direction, we need to develop criteria for evaluating other churches and, indeed, for reevaluating our own.[2] Our vision for reunion should not include every organization that calls itself a Christian church. There are certainly bodies using that name—The Church of Jesus Christ of Latter-Day Saints, for example—that are not Christian churches and they should have no role to play in any ecumenical venture. Our goal is reunion of the one, *true* church.

What Is a True Church?

But what *is* a true church? And what denominations are suitable candidates for mergers? The Protestant Reformers suggested three criteria for a sound church: the true preaching of the Word of God, the right administration of the sacraments, and the diligent exercise of church discipline. Although I believe that these criteria may be misleading without some explication or even supplementation, I will begin by considering these. As I do, I would remind you of an earlier point: that Scripture requires Christians to give one another the benefit of the doubt. If a church claims to be a Christian church, that claim ought to be accepted unless there is cogent reason for rejecting it. The burden of proof is upon those who would reject such claims. It is remarkable that through church history, though there have been many schisms, it has been very rare that one denomination has accused another of total apostasy.[3] The Protestant Reformers did not take that position in regard to the Roman Catholic Church, nor do many denominations today take such views of their rivals. Thus, we may expect the burden of proof to be very heavy indeed. In fact, as we shall see, it is.

The True Preaching of the Word of God

One's view of what constitutes true preaching of the Word will depend somewhat on one's theological perspective. Yet it would be wrong to insist that that preaching must agree with one's own theology in every detail to constitute true preaching.[4] As I argued earlier, some degree of tolerance is inevitable. How much? Here I can only refer the reader to the less-than-definitive suggestions of chapter 8.

My personal application of those scriptural principles comes about as I ask my conscience before God whether this or that deserves to be called authentic gospel preaching. There is an inevitable subjective dimension to any application of scriptural principles.[5] This is not subjectiv-*ism*, because (1) it is an application *of scriptural principle;* (2) it is the divinely ordained route to *truth;* and (3) each individual's decision ought to be open to correction from others in the church: God leads his people corporately by his Spirit.

In my own (Presbyterian) circles, the discussion often centers around the question of whether Arminians preach an authentic gospel. I hope my Arminian readers will not be too upset if I take this as a serious question and seek to answer it. In return, I will not offended if some Arminian writer asks the same question about Calvinistic preaching, especially if, as in my discussion below, he comes to an affirmative conclusion. I want to deal with Arminianism at this point simply so I may illustrate the kind of thinking that we must do to assess one another according to biblical standards.

Some Calvinists think that there is in effect no truth in Arminianism, that it is in fact equivalent to paganism because it fails to affirm a fully sovereign God.[6] I agree with these Calvinists that the Arminian doctrine of free will is in error, and that if all the rest of Arminian theology were worked out to be consistent with that error, the result would be paganism.[7]

However: (1) Arminian theology is not, in my judgment, developed with a view toward consistency with that error, and indeed it does not achieve such consistency. It is therefore, at worst, an inconsistent theology, not a pagan theology.[8] And (2) The error in question occurs mostly in technical discussions, not in preaching or in popular theology. Technically, Arminians regard human free decisions (at least the decision to believe in Christ) as causeless and independent of God's decrees. But when Arminian *preachers* bring up the issue of free will (which, to be sure, they do) they tend to use formulations that can be construed as an authentic biblical doctrine of human responsibility. Calvinism, too, teaches "human responsibility" and means by this phrase that human faith—a real, uncoerced, and meaningful choice that only the individual can make—is necessary and important to salvation. Most of the Arminian preaching I have heard does not go beyond this picture of human responsibility. I often wonder if the Calvinistic critics of Arminianism are fully aware of what Calvin and the Reformed confessions themselves teach about human responsibility, even about "free will"!

It is true that Calvinism teaches the total inability of man to do anything toward his salvation. Wesleyan preachers, however, because of their view of "prevenient grace" often tell the unbeliever that he *is* "able" to come to Jesus, to make a decision for Christ. Here, however, let us note that there are many kinds of "ability." What the Calvinist denies is that the unbeliever has the *moral* ability to make the right choice apart from saving (not merely "prevenient") grace. He "cannot" decide to obey Christ, because he cannot do anything that is morally right. On the other hand, even on the Calvinistic view, there are senses in which the unbeliever "can" make the right decision: (1) he has, usually,[9] the mental ability to understand the choice before him and to make the right decision; (2) he has, usually, the physical ability to do the things that please God; (3) he is not prevented, by elements of his heredity or environment, from pleasing God; (4) God's offer in the gospel to save those who come to him by faith is a sincere one; those who come to Christ he will not cast out (John 6:37). The need for grace is genuine, but it is a need that God meets. So no one can plead lack of grace as an excuse for failing to believe in Christ.

Preachers rarely make these distinctions. In preaching it is not a matter of whether the hearer has this or that kind of ability, but simply of whether he "can" or "cannot" properly respond to the message. Some Calvinist preachers go out of their way to inform the unbeliever that he "cannot" come to Christ; Arminians typically seek to inform him that he "can," and that he is therefore responsible to do so. Faced with those two alternatives, I am inclined to think that the Arminian presentation is more biblical! I say that, even though I reject the Arminian theory of prevenient grace and free will by which the Arminian technical theology justifies such preaching. To tell unbelievers that they "cannot" come to Christ, while true in a sense, is to encourage passivity on their part. It tells them to wait and see if God will do something to them. That is not the biblical pattern, which, without neglecting the necessity of grace,[10] rather stresses present responsibility and encourages action. On the other hand, the Arminian pattern of telling unbelievers that they "can" come to Christ and are therefore responsible is true in a sense and does properly encourage a response of faith.

Would it not be better if evangelists made the proper distinctions between different kinds of ability before making their appeal? Such a suggestion does not indicate a proper understanding of the evangelistic situation. It bids us include very technical theological distinctions in teaching that is directed to people with no biblical discernment.

My own conclusion, then, is that Arminian preaching is far better than Arminian theology, better even than some of the worst forms of Calvinistic preaching. If now and then more serious errors enter Arminian sermons, I must be honest and recognize that serious errors often enter Calvinistic sermons as well.

I would have no difficulty inviting a non-Christian friend to hear the gospel from an Arminian evangelist or from one who, like Billy Graham, does not draw the theological lines between the two very sharply. While I would certainly prefer for myself and family to hear Calvinistic preaching (not at its worst, but at its average or better) as our steady diet, I have no hesitation in admitting that Arminian preachers, on the average, do preach the biblical gospel.

This is the kind of mutual analysis I am recommending: discerning and analytical, but sympathetic; not taking historical polemics for granted, but seeking to penetrate beneath those polemics to identify otherwise hidden areas of unity—or diversity. It is a form of analysis that seeks not only to identify differences, but also to assess the weight of those differences, to see them in proper perspective.

I cannot, however, leave the subject of true preaching without touching on some other areas. The discussion above pertains mostly to doctrinal assessment. But it is also important to evaluate preaching as to effectiveness, balance of content, style, and other matters. A preacher can be perfectly orthodox and yet be a poor communicator. If he fails to get the gospel across to real people, can his preaching be called "true preaching of the Word"? I doubt it. Preaching is a form of communication; where communication is lacking, preaching is not really preaching.

Or a preacher can be perfectly orthodox and yet be hung up on certain "hobby horses," certain pet topics that he preaches constantly to the exclusion of other important biblical truth. That is potentially at least as dangerous as theological error. Or a preacher may be so negative in his style and formulations that he fails utterly to communicate the joy and freedom of the gospel. That, too, is a falsification.

Preaching that presupposes an "ingrown" as opposed to "outward facing" view of the church is a very serious deformity, for it implicitly renounces the church's fundamental task set forth in Matthew 28:19–20.

On these criteria, much preaching that appears quite adequate from a traditional theological analysis comes off looking very bad. I cannot say, as some would, that the traditional theological criteria are the most important; because these latter criteria are theological as well. They have to do with our obedience or disobedience to God's word.[11]

This is why I said earlier that I have sometimes recommended for inquirers to sit under ministries committed to traditions other than the Presbyterian. The question is "How much truth actually gets across?" In my judgment, it is often the case that more truth actually gets across in non-Reformed preaching than in Reformed preaching.

I do believe that if we engaged in this kind of analysis, we would find more faults in our own traditions and more virtues in the traditions of others. So much the better for the prospects of reunion!

The Right Administration of the Sacraments

On this criterion, compare chapter 9, in which I argued a fairly liberal view of sacramental acceptance of Christians from other denominations. The main tradition of the church has been to accept as valid the sacraments of schismatics and some "heretics," even when there are some errors in the theology and administration of those sacraments.[12] Of course, recognizing validity of a church's baptism, for instance, is not the same thing as agreeing with that church's theology of baptism. Although I seriously disagree with both Roman Catholics and Baptists as to their theology of baptism, I do not deny that people baptized under such auspices are truly baptized. These are both churches that hold to the Nicene-Constantinopolitan Creed of 381, and they are doing what Jesus commanded to initiate members of the church. They may think they are doing much more, or they may deny additional elements of the sacrament that I would affirm. But I cannot deny that they are certainly baptizing, whatever else they may or may not be doing. I would not personally participate in a Roman Catholic baptismal ceremony, for I would not want to imply consent to much of what is being said. But I cannot deny that one who receives baptism, even in such a ceremony, is truly baptized.

Similarly with the Lord's Supper. I agree with the Protestant Reformers that the Roman mass is blasphemous, because in it there is idolatrous worship of the host (thought to be the literal body of Christ) and because the mass is regarded as some sort of continuing sacrifice for sin. These are serious errors, and they would prevent me from participating in Roman Catholic communion unless I could get assurance that those doctrines were not held by the particular congregation in question. Yet I do not deny that in such circumstances the Lord's Supper is being received. Think of a parallel with preaching (for the Reformers usefully regarded the sacraments as "visible words"): A sermon may contain a mixture of error and truth; yet the presence of error does not prove that the truth has not also been present.

Church Discipline

The third mark of the church is that which maintains the presence of the other two. I have mentioned earlier (chapter 4) that discipline is very much on the wane today in the church for many reasons, among them denominationalism itself. Very few churches actually have formal judicial processes to discipline, especially to excommunicate those who are involved in sin, even though Scripture clearly provides for them (Matt. 18:15–20; 1 Cor. 5; etc.).

The absence of *formal* discipline does not mean that discipline is totally absent. Teaching and counseling are themselves forms of discipline. And churches do have informal ways of making unrepentant adulterers, for example, feel rebuked, even to the point of driving them from the fellowship. This sort of approach is not the best kind of discipline. It is surely better in most cases to have formal procedures available, in addition to the informal process of mutual admonition and rebuke. That way, such matters can be dealt with fairly and in order, rather than allowing gossip and prejudice to go unimpeded, as so often happens in "informal" discipline. But informal discipline *is* discipline nonetheless.

And in many cases informal discipline may be preferable to a formal procedure that is harsh, arbitrary, impatient, or unloving. Even in the case of excommunication, the goal of church discipline is always to restore the offender (1 Cor. 5:5).

Most orthodox churches (judging "orthodoxy" roughly according to the creed of 381) have enough discipline, formal or informal, to maintain their doctrinal and moral integrity from one generation to the next. We may well wish for more, but the question before us is the minimal definition of a true church. In fairness, I doubt that we will be able to remove many bodies from the list of true churches by reference to the mark of discipline. I would say that the major liberal denominations, as national organizations, lack this mark; or, worse, they use discipline to punish orthodoxy and to enforce error. An example of the latter, in my opinion, would be the requirement of the Presbyterian Church, U.S.A. that its officers support the ordination of women. But even to say this is not to deny that legitimate discipline exists in these denominations, at least at the congregational and middle (presbyterial, synodical) levels.

Other Marks?

The three traditional marks of the church are still a fairly good guide for us to determine what bodies are and are not true churches. However, unless they are accompanied by elaborate explanation, they do not adequately characterize the distinctive qualities of the New Testament church as it stands overagainst the world. For one thing, the traditional marks do not specify the unique task to which the church is called (Matt. 28:19f). The Great Commission may, to be sure, be seen as implicit in the other marks, especially that of teaching, as we have seen. But to speak merely of "teaching" may well encourage the ingrownness of the church, which I criticized earlier.

Earlier in this chapter, I did indicate what *kind* of "teaching" must be done to do justice to the Great Commission. Here, let me go beyond that and say that the entire ministry of the church is to be outward-facing, geared to the salvation of the lost and their training to be mature members of the body. A church that is not preoccupied with reaching the unsaved is not merely a weak church; it is not properly a church at all.

Another mark neglected in the usual enumeration is the mark Jesus mentioned when he said, "By this all men will know that you are my disciples, if you love one another" (John 13:35). Earlier I mentioned that discipline ought to be loving. But much more needs to be said here. Love, according to Jesus, is *the* mark; it is *the* means by which Christians are to be distinguished from the world. Paul's way of putting it is also instructive: whatever gifts we have—whether prophecy, tongues, knowledge, faith, generosity—none has any meaning without love (1 Cor. 13:1–3; cf. 1 John 2:10f; 3:14–18, 23; 4:7–21).

Evaluating churches by this mark is bound to involve some element of subjectivity. That is true to some extent of all evaluation, but especially here. Nevertheless, I am very reluctant to recognize as a true church a church where discipline is harsh or mechanical, where the worst features of bureaucracy[13] dominate the administrative structure, where preaching is largely denunciatory, where people have a haughty, prideful, or suspicious attitude toward Christians outside their group, where there is no ministry to the poor, where the shepherds beat the sheep rather than feeding and gently leading.

What Church Should I Join?

We should only join "true" churches, defined according to all the marks listed above. Beyond that, God's word allows us considerable latitude.

In some cases, even a true church will err in such a way as to be undeserving of new members. For instance, if a church requires one to do something he or she regards as sinful as a criterion of membership (supporting abortion, for example, or supporting theologically liberal colleges, seminaries, missionaries), a believer should not join this church.

Otherwise, many criteria may play a role. It is natural for a Christian to seek a church that agrees with his doctrinal position. Most of us don't believe that we will receive excellent teaching unless the teachers of the church interpret Scripture pretty much the way we do. For example, if one is a Baptist, and the local Baptist churches lack evangelistic vision and/or mutual love, Scripture certainly permits this believer to look elsewhere.

Geography, quality of programs for youth and children, depth of worship, and quality of pastoral care all play legitimate roles in our choices. It is wrong, however, to make a choice purely or largely on the basis of denominational affiliation. Indeed, denominational affiliation as such is not a biblical criterion, for denominations play no role in New Testament church government (see chapter 1). We ought to cultivate an openness to crossing denominational lines when doing that will best meet the spiritual needs of our families and ourselves.

What Is a Good Candidate for Church Union?

I can accept most evangelical Arminian churches as true churches, but I would not advocate at this time seeking merger between them and my own denomination.[14] Such a merger would take many years of negotiations, and the prospect of reaching sufficient unity of mind to merge is extremely dim. Since we must use our energies in the way most helpful to the kingdom and to church unity, it makes sense first to seek union with those who are closest to us. Presbyterians should seek union with other Presbyterians, Wesleyans with other Wesleyans, Baptists with other Baptists, and so on.[15]

Eventually we wish to merge with all who love the Lord and who demonstrate that love by a profession of faith made credible by their lives. Who does that include? Could, for example, a united evangelical denomination ever consider merger with the Roman Catholic Church? Well, by the time we need to cross that bridge, the Roman Catholic Church might have changed a great deal! If it has not changed, however, I would regard it as I regard the large liberal Protestant denominations: there are many Christians in these organizations, perhaps godly congregations and regional units as well. But right now I believe the organization as a whole is committed to so many serious errors that it is not a fit candidate for merger into the one, true church. Christians within the church, perhaps even congregations and bishoprics, may be candidates, but not the denomination as a whole.

Notes

1. COCU stood originally for "Consultation on Church Union," later for "Church of Christ Uniting." This movement was set up to implement the vision of Eugene Carson Blake. Stated Clerk of the PCUSA, and James Pike, Bishop of the Protestant Episcopal Church, to merge the major United States denominations into one.

2. In this section I am thinking about evaluating churches, not denominations as such, though we must also learn to evaluate denominations by the same criteria. One complicating factor is that there can be sound churches in unsound denominations. One can well argue that they ought not to be in those denominations; but one cannot doubt that this sort of thing happens. So, to say that a denomination (as a national organization) is apostate or not a true manifestation

of the church is not necessarily to say that all its presbyteries, dioceses, congregations, ministers, or members are apostate. Those must be evaluated separately.

3. An "apostate" church is a body that was once a church but can no longer legitimately be called a church.

4. If that were the case, I doubt if I could accept any preaching as true except my own, and even my own past preaching would be of very doubtful integrity.

5. See my Doctrine of the Knowledge of God (Phillipsburg, N.J.: Presbyterian and Reformed, 1987), pp. 76–88, 149–164, 319–346.

6. To see this view presented in its most extreme form, note the discussion in Journey magazine between William Dennison, William White, and myself, in various articles, letters, and replies in the issues of Sept.-Oct. 1987, March-April 1988, May-June 1988, July-Oct. 1988, Jan.-Feb. 1989. The position I oppose in these exchanges I would characterize as theological chauvinism (a close cousin of denominationalism) at its worst.

7. Indeed, most all theological errors, worked out consistently, lead to paganism, including the ones of which I—or you—may be guilty.

8. These analyses of Arminianism (like other such analyses in this book) are certainly not rigorous enough to be persuasive as they stand, at least to one who is inclined to doubt them. Nor have I taken the trouble to document them. To do so would be to distract us from our purpose, which is not to prove any conclusion about Arminianism, but rather to present an illustration of how someone might think through questions about what is or is not a true church.

9. The qualification pertains to those who because of youth, retardation, brain damage, and the like cannot understand the message. I cannot here enter into the problems raised by such cases.

10. Does Arminian preaching neglect the necessity of grace? One would not know it from John Wesley's sermons, or from Charles Wesley's wonderful "And Can It Be?"

11. It is only in this broadened sense that we ought to accept "true preaching of the Word" as a mark of the true church. If we take the phrase as referring only to the theoretical orthodoxy of the preacher, we will be mistaken as to what Scripture really expects of the true church.

12. We should always remember that error is a matter of degree. No one's sacramental theology or practice is perfect; no one's is wrong in every respect.

13. In general, bureaucracy at its worst looks like this: The official is proud, more interested in guarding his (or her) turf than in serving the people (contra Matt. 20:26–28). He insists on "procedures," even when they hurt people, even when they disrupt rather than help the progress of the church's ministry. Such officials must have all the forms signed, with i's dotted and t's crossed, because they must never be inconvenienced in the work of bookkeeping. At worst, the bureaucrat will impose a major inconvenience on someone else in order to maintain a minor convenience for himself.

14. Except, possibly, via joint membership in a kind of evangelical COCU (see first paragraph of this chapter).

15. On the other hand, one of my correspondents (a Presbyterian) suggests that it might be better if we just dissolved the Presbyterian churches and send their members out to join other churches. I suggested in an earlier context that Presbyterian churches tend to have a higher percentage of good teachers than other denominations, while being relatively deficient in other gifts. On my correspondent's proposal, the Presbyterian teachers could influence other bodies in the direction of union. Well, perhaps all our denominations should be dissolved, and we should just scramble ourselves up again, perhaps forming congregations along neighborhood lines. Like "back to the future," this is an unrealistic proposal that I really don't want to advocate. But it does stimulate the mind in radical directions!

16

················

Guidelines
for Church Union

When we find a likely candidate for reunion, what then? I cannot here suggest a very specific set of steps; that will vary from case to case. But let me suggest a perspective that ought to guide us through the often difficult process of bringing churches back together.

Church Union as Reunion and Reconciliation

I have been using the phrases *church union* and *merger* because of their familiarity and because I wanted to postpone some refinements to these concepts until this point in the book. Actually I prefer to speak, as I have from time to time, of *reunion* rather than union. This is to keep reminding ourselves that organizational church union is not something that we are seeking to create for the first time. Rather, it was created by Jesus Christ and, at least in its organizational dimension, destroyed by the sins of human beings. That disunity has been perpetuated by sinful attitudes and practices of which all of us have probably in some measure and at some times been guilty. What we seek now, therefore, is most precisely described *not* as union but as reunion.

The particular kind of reunion we are speaking about involves rec-onciliation. We are apart because of sin, or at least because of percep-tions of sin (recall chapter 11). Scripture tells us that when someone sins against us (Matt. 18:15ff), or when someone rightly or wrongly perceives that we have sinned against him (Matt. 5:23ff), we must go to that person and try to straighten things out. Scripture puts such a high priority on reconciliation that it tells us to interrupt an act of worship if necessary to accomplish it (cf. Eph. 4:26: "Do not let the sun go down while you are still angry . . ."). If reconciliation has such a high priority in Scripture, certainly church reunion, a form of recon-ciliation, also has a high priority. Church reunion is not a luxury that we can postpone indefinitely; it is a sore need of the church today (recall Part One).

In the (lamentably defunct) *Presbyterian Journal,*[1] there was an article entitled "Yes, But Can She Cook?" which compared church-union discussions to courtship and suggested a thorough analysis of one another's strengths and weaknesses before any union could take place. The courtship metaphor is a common one in discussions of any kind of "merger," ecclesiastical or corporate. That metaphor does add some vividness and sometimes refreshing levity to the discussion. And it does describe well the kind of thinking that, alas, usually dominates discussions of church union. But we must remember that it is *only* a metaphor and, in one sense, a deeply misleading one. Church union is not "courtship." It is reconciliation after illegitimate separation. A much better family metaphor would be the remarriage of a couple who had sinfully divorced.[2]

"Yes, but can she cook?" is a question appropriate to courtship. Since a single person normally has no divine obligation to marry any other particular person, he or she has the luxury of being able to care-fully scrutinize all the strengths and weaknesses of any marriage candi-date. Thus, any number of things, cooking included, may be sufficient to postpone or cancel the wedding plans. In most circumstances, there is nothing obligatory or urgent about such a marriage.

But the situation is very different in the case of two people who have sinfully divorced. They *must* remarry; God requires it.[3] Since rec-onciliation is involved, the matter is *urgent,* not to be delayed. People in this position do not have the luxury of sorting out all of each other's strengths and weaknesses, as if, say, the man could forego remarriage if he decided his wife was not intelligent enough. They must remarry whether or not the remarriage appears to be wise from the standpoint of human calculation. They must remarry even though they might now prefer to remain single or to choose another partner. They must remarry even if their human wisdom concludes that remarriage would weaken them or frustrate them in some way.

In the reconciliation model, "Yes, but can she cook?" is a tragically inappropriate question. Imagine a sinfully divorced man refusing reconciliation on the ground that he doesn't like his wife's cooking. We can see how different is the courtship model from the divorce/reconciliation model of church reunion. The courtship model denies the urgency and the obligation of reunion. It pictures church union as something we can take or leave, depending on even minor personal preferences. The reconciliation model, on the other hand, reflects Jesus' passion for the unity of his body.

On the reconciliation model, church union may not be refused—except for the sake of conscience. That one qualification is necessary. Some union invitations, after all, come with strings attached; they require or render likely certain changes in doctrine or practice that an individual, church, or denomination cannot accept in good conscience. We cannot enter any body where we will be required to sin as a condition of continued membership in good standing. Such invitations are not true opportunities for reunion; they do not rebuild the church that Jesus established. But, with that one exception, we must affirm the implication of the reconciliation model: *We must accept any union proposal that we can accept in good conscience.*

Burden of Proof

Because of the "exception" noted above, union is never a foregone conclusion. Any church or denomination contemplating union must do some thinking about it first. But that thinking should be limited to consideration of whether there are any *barriers to conscience* in the proposed union. The question is not whether we will be strengthened or weakened by a union,[4] but whether we will commit sin by entering into it.

The question, then, is not "Why merge?" but "Why *not* merge?" Our job is negative, rather than positive: to look for conscientious obstacles to union, not to look for reasons to unite. That means that the burden of proof is always on the *opponents* of union. This fits the biblical pattern we observed earlier in this book. In Scripture, people are innocent until proven guilty. The burden of proof is always on the prosecution. Union discussions are much like judicial trials in that opponents of union are in fact accusing the other denomination of some error or sin that would prevent union. They must bear the burden of proof and present convincing evidence. *Otherwise, the union must be accepted.*

I cannot express this point too strongly. Let me reiterate it by sharing an experience. In 1986, the OPC General Assembly discussed whether they should unite with the PCA. I was a commissioner, and I made a speech contending for the above point, that commissioners should vote *for* the union unless they were persuaded on conscientious grounds not to do so. I emphasized that the burden of proof was on the opponents of union and argued the point somewhat as I have here. Later a fellow elder stood up and made a speech in which he argued the opposite: that those in doubt about the union should play it safe, in effect, by voting against it. He may have used Romans 14:23: ". . . everything that does not come from faith is sin." The elder did not refer at all to my previous speech and made no attempt to reply to my arguments; therefore I did not take him very seriously and made no attempt to reply. But, after the union vote failed, a number of men told me (to my astonishment, I confess) that my fellow elder's speech had greatly influenced the decision.

If that sort of reasoning is persuasive to any of my readers, let me reply now as I should have replied then: *Scripture puts the burden of proof on the opponents of union.* Therefore, if someone is in doubt about union with another denomination, he must resolve that doubt in favor of the union. To do otherwise than follow Scripture is not to "play it safe"; it is to invite upon ourselves the fatherly discipline of God, which can at times be very severe. As for Romans 14:23, an anti-union vote contrary to scriptural criteria *cannot* be done "from faith." *Voting against union in such circumstances is sin.*

One more point about burden of proof. Bearing this burden means taking responsibility for the quality of evidence presented. I have often been appalled at the amount of gossip, unsubstantiated rumor, and such that is presented as evidence in discussions of church union. In a judicial trial of an individual, whether civil or ecclesiastical, the court would be subject to rules of evidence, cross-examination would be allowed, replies to all allegations would be solicited, unclear matters clarified. But in union discussions, all these safeguards are typically absent, and discussion proceeds as if anything that comes to mind can be said, no matter what harm to people or loss of truth. This is sin, which would be obvious if an individual were being excommunicated on the basis of such flimsy evidence. But to reject a union is in effect to excommunicate an entire denomination! Yet we accept extremely low standards of evidence in such serious deliberations. In my view, church-union discussions ought to be conducted with judicial formality, with representatives of the other body invited to reply to allegations, and strict rules of evidence.

Non-Conscience Problems

I have said that we should support unions except where conscience prevents us. What about those problems that are not really problems of *conscience*, but that nevertheless make unions difficult to achieve? Say that we disagree strongly with the way the other denomination finances its missions efforts. Or that we do not particularly like the Sunday school materials produced by the other group. Or that we don't want to be assessed to support its college. Should issues like these prevent or postpone reunion? Many, certainly, would want at least to negotiate such matters before agreeing to unite.

But what does God say? Again, imagine a sinfully divorced husband and wife "negotiating" their remarriage. Since the divorce, the wife has acquired some drapes that the husband doesn't care for; or her obnoxious brother has come to live in the house; or she has had an ugly house addition built over the husband's back-yard putting green. Must all these matters be worked out before remarriage? God says no; remarriage is a biblical norm. Then how are these differences to be resolved? Within the marriage, of course. The couple should remarry even if they cannot agree on all these secondary matters. Then they should work out the problems (under the headship of the husband, I believe), in openness to the counsel of the church if necessary.

The same goes for church unions. What is God's method for resolving disputes over such secondary matters as mission financing and support of colleges? The deliberation and government of the church, of course. In my presbyterian theology, such decisions are made—at appropriate levels and with provision for appeal—by local sessions, presbyteries, synods, and general assemblies. Other governmental systems have different ways of doing it. But clearly the way to resolve these matters is not to shout at one another over man-made denominational barriers or to throw out ultimatums that unless this or that changes we will not unite.

Another fellow elder who opposed the OPC-PCA union argued that much more discussion was needed over the sorts of matters described in the last two paragraphs. He felt that failure to discuss these matters amounted to submission to a "corporate takeover," that is, simply letting the other church take us over on its terms. In a sense he was right. That particular union would have submerged our tiny OPC (20,000 members) in the much larger PCA (200,000 members), so that the larger church surely would have had the deciding voice in any matter on which the two bodies differed. My fellow elder favored more negotiations, agreements as conditions of union, and promises that on at least some matters things would be done *our* way.

My reply: What my fellow elder was asking for was really quite undemocratic and unpresbyterian. Had we merged with the PCA, we would have remained elders, members of various church courts in which we would have been entitled to one vote each. In effect, the former OPC people would have one vote to the ten of those who had been in the PCA. That is only fair; in the presbyterian system, one elder has one vote. On the basis of such votes, the various issues could have been resolved. What my fellow elder was asking for was something more than "one man, one vote." He was asking to have an influence out of proportion to his actual status as *one* elder in the church of Christ. He was demanding that the majority accept minority positions as a condition of union. That is hardly even remotely fair, let alone scriptural. Of course, church constitutions, like civil ones, frequently contain special considerations for minority rights, and that is often proper. But even those can fairly be determined only by majority vote.

God's way is that such issues should be resolved *in* the church, not over pre-merger negotiation tables. The proper order is first to unite, if we can do so in good conscience, and then to deal with those problems that are not matters of conscience.

Problems of Conscience

I have said that we should reject mergers that would involve us in sin. What sorts of things do I have in mind?

In discussing the nature of a true church (chapter 12), I used, with some supplements and explications, the Reformation criteria of the preaching of the Word, administration of the sacraments, and discipline. Certainly, if a merger proposal is not to create problems of conscience, it must involve nothing but true churches. But, beyond this, recall that many true churches have fallen prey to serious errors in doctrine and practice. I would not advocate union with any body that required me to teach error or to do something I regard as sinful.

To give an example, I would never advocate that my PCA merge with the large, mostly liberal Presbyterian Church, U.S.A. Though I grant that there are many godly people in the latter denomination and, indeed, some fine congregations, I and my fellow PCA elders could not conscientiously accept the present requirements of PCUSA eldership. For example, the PCUSA requires elders to subscribe to a Book of Confessions, including the Confession of 1967 that legitimizes Barthian theology within the church. Further, the weakness of the ordination vows in the PCUSA raise questions about whether any substantial (formal!) theological discipline can be accomplished within that denomination. And the denomination requires ministers to participate in the ordination of women elders, which I and most in the PCA believe to be an unscriptural practice.[5]

If it were possible to protest these "unscriptural practices" within the PCUSA with reasonable hope that the policies might be reversed in the exercise of ecclesiastical discipline, it would not be wrong for us to join the PCUSA—while conscientiously refusing to follow its policies in these areas—assuming that they would accept us as members under such conditions. But we should recall that the mark of "discipline" is needed to reverse such errors. The important question, then, is whether there is adequate discipline in the PCUSA to reverse these errors. At the moment I am inclined to say no.

In a sense, then, questions about the Word and sacraments reduce to questions about discipline. If there is sufficient discipline, errors in the other areas can be dealt with; if there is not sufficient discipline, even agreements on the Word and sacraments cannot be expected to continue.

Therefore, the most important question when contemplating merger is, *"Can we trust the courts of a united denomination?"* If we *can* trust the courts of a united denomination, we can work out disagreements of doctrine and practice, together with the more trivial kinds of concerns, the "Yes, but can she cook?" questions discussed in the last section. If that italicized question can be answered yes, then we ought to unite; if not, then no, at least for now. In my view, then, this is the *only* question that ought to be "on the table" prior to merger. All other questions, insofar as they have some legitimacy, are wrapped up in this one.

Joining and Receiving

Some years ago, representatives of three small Presbyterian bodies (OPC, PCA, RPCES) met to discuss the possibility of union. It was assumed that if these bodies wished to unite, they would first have to go through a period of negotiation to determine the nature of the new united church. No one looked forward to such negotiations; typically they would take years, deal with all sorts of trivia, seek to overcome all sorts of petty objections. But one representative at the meeting had a bright idea and asked the others, "What if we simply asked to *join* you?" The idea caught on, and the concept of "joining and receiving" was born. Indeed, that concept led to union between RPCES and PCA in 1981. The OPC was left out of the 1981 union but was given a second chance, which it turned down in 1986.[6]

"J&R" is an exciting concept, one that fits very well into the reconciliation model I have been advocating. It says: If you can do it conscientiously, then simply join, and afterward work out your problems, as God intended, in the councils of the church, not around an interdenominational negotiating table. It is a promising model for those situations in which problems of conscience are not likely to be raised, usually where two or more denominations are very close to one another in doctrine and practice. In general I find it far superior to the negotiating-table procedure, for both theological and practical reasons. It is faster, more efficient than the other, as well as adequately representing the biblical urgency of union.

The joining-and-receiving idea does not necessarily succeed, of course. The 1986 attempt failed because some in the OPC developed (in my view, unjustified) problems of conscience, and because others elevated nonconscientious problems to an unbiblically high priority. But it was a worthy attempt, and I would recommend consideration of it in other evangelical circles.[7]

Notes

1. Jan. 21, 1981

2. Even this metaphor is not strong enough. For often in divorce, even when one spouse is sinful in divorcing the other, the other spouse is free to remarry the original partner or not. See John Murray, *Divorce* (Grand Rapids: Baker, 1961). But, in the ecclesiastical case, both parties have an obligation to reunite if such reunion does not otherwise violate God's will.

3. With the qualification mentioned in the previous footnote.

4. If another denomination is weaker than ourselves (and of course our judgments in these matters are very fallible), our obligation is not to abandon it to its own resources; rather our obligation is to add our resources to it. Union with a weaker body should be seen as a joyous opportunity to help our weaker brothers and sisters.

5. Indeed, the denomination *requires* congregations to elect a certain quota of women elders. PCUSA discipline is, in my view, extremely weak in enforcing biblical orthodoxy, but very strong in enforcing this *unbiblical* practice.

6. Actually a majority of the assembly voted in favor of union, but a two-thirds vote was required, and the total was considerably lower than that proportion.

7. It was to the J&R method of union that my friend mentioned earlier objected, claiming it was like a "corporate takeover." I still believe my reply to him was sufficient.

17

❊ ❊

May We Ever
Leave a Church?

After all this emphasis on the importance of unity, some readers may be troubled with the question of whether one is ever justified in leaving one church or denomination to join another. You might think I believe (as some have written) that a person must stay in the church he is in for the rest of his life, barring a geographical move of some distance.

Actually, however, my view is toward the opposite extreme. I believe that there are many legitimate reasons for moving between churches and between denominations. Indeed, I believe in very liberal emigration procedures. The walls between denominations and churches ought to be very low. My hope is that so many will move back and forth from one denomination to another that in time it will be difficult to tell the denominations apart!

As to the justifications for such transfers, I have referred to them from time to time in earlier chapters, but I would like to present them more explicitly here. In a sense this chapter is something of a digression, not part of the overall argument in favor of church union. Those who want to follow the argument narrowly defined should skip this material and move on to the next chapter. I do, however, feel some obligation to pause here to gather together some loose ends. So, as in the last chapter I gave some "Guidelines for Church Union," I will in this chapter give some "Guidelines for Church Division."

When is it permissible to leave one body and join another? First, I believe that it is almost never right to leave one denomination to *start* a new one. There are plenty of denominations around already! These have a wide variety of theologies, practices, styles. Surely one is not being very thoughtful if he cannot find a single one that honors his concerns. Why should we ever create a *new division* in the body of Christ, a *new* barrier to reunion?

In terms of the above principle, I believe that both OPC and PCA have erred. Both denominations broke away from their previous denominations and started new ones. Neither was justified, in my view. The founders of the OPC, granted that they had just cause to leave the PCUSA, could have joined the Christian Reformed Church, the United Presbyterian Church of North America, the Reformed Presbyterian Church General Synod, the Associate Reformed Presbyterian Church, or others. The founders of the PCA could have joined the already existing OPC or some of the other bodies mentioned. (The United Presbyterian Church of North America no longer existed when the PCA founders left the PCUS.)

Why did they not join already existing bodies? Hard to say. My guess is that they did not want to endure the shock of the unfamiliar in addition to the other shocks they were receiving. They wanted a fellowship pretty much like the one they left, minus the grievance that brought the break. That motive, of course, is not scriptural.

The *argument* they used, however, was this: "Our previous denomination, whether through apostasy as such or just through committing grave sin, has relinquished its right to the allegiance of God's people. It is our purpose to be the *continuance* of our former denomination's testimony." Thus, one of the early names for the PCA was the Continuing Presbyterian Church. To be the "continuing" body, they could not join some already existing denomination.

I hesitate to describe this argument as a bad one, pure and simple. I suspect it would have seemed a lot more plausible to me if I had been in on the founding of one of these denominations. Yet, at this moment, while I understand the sentiment underlying this concept, I must reject it as unbiblical. Scripture does not call us to "continue" the testimony of old, wasted denominations. It simply calls us to testify for Jesus. The PCUS, of which the PCA saw itself a "continuance," was itself a mere denomination, a split in Jesus' body. A split in Jesus' body is not a fit subject for Christian celebration, or even perpetuation. The PCUS and the PCUSA broke with one another during the Civil War. That split should not have occurred, in my opinion.[1] Therefore, in my view, the PCUS should never have existed. It does not deserve to be "continued" by its evangelical successor.[2]

If there are any exceptions to this rule, I do not know of them. Therefore, I would urge those who have good reasons for leaving a church body to join an already existing denomination rather than starting a new one.

But, when *is* it legitimate to leave one church/denomination and join another? I think there are many legitimate reasons, but also many potential dangers.

In many cases, such transfer is a minor matter. When a church member is transferred to another city and for some reason or other prefers to join a church of a different denomination (one fairly close to the first in doctrine and practice), he or she rarely undergoes any criticism. When the pastor of a church accepts a call to be pastor of a church in a different denomination (again, of the same doctrinal family), he rarely arouses any opposition. That is the way it ought to be. Denominations are not New Testament institutions, but divisions *imposed on* the New Testament church. In the New Testament, apostles, prophets, and church workers (like Aquila and Priscilla) moved freely from place to place, ministering to different churches. We should have the same freedom to do that today, even when such moves require us to cross denominational barriers.

People sometimes argue that interdenominational transfer is a breaking of vows or a betrayal of fellowship, but I cannot see any value in that argument. Of course, people often take vows when they join a church, but those vows never include the promise that one will remain a member of that church/denomination for life. Nor is one who seeks transfer necessarily "betraying" anything, anymore than did the apostle Paul when he said good-bye to the Ephesian elders and went on to Jerusalem.

It is sometimes said (indeed, I once used to say this) that one ought not to transfer to escape from some interpersonal problem in the church. It is true that people sometimes leave a church to avoid having to confront a brother or sister about a difficult situation, according to Matthew 5 and 18. That of course is wrong. We must settle our differences in biblical ways. Still, one can settle differences with a brother in a biblical way without remaining in the same congregation or denomination with him. Thus, whether there are unresolved interpersonal problems is irrelevant to the question of whether someone can or should leave.

I also once said that one should never leave a church or denomination to flee possible discipline. But I have also changed my view on that matter. When someone is under discipline by one denomination, he has the right to appeal to the Christian church beyond that denominational limit, just as during the New Testament period there were (I believe) courts of the whole church to which such a one might take his case. When someone under discipline leaves one church to join another, he is in effect making an "appeal" of his conviction to another part of the body of Christ. That second part may uphold the initial discipline, or they may question it. In either case, it seems to me that justice is being done, albeit in a very imperfect way.

I also used to say that one should never leave a church if that church needs him or her to survive. But, from God's point of view, no human being is indispensable. If God wants a weak church to keep going, he will supply the gifts that church needs. On the other hand, I have come to the view that it is not a tragedy when a tiny, stagnant, sick church folds up and dies. It is better for the members of such churches to be part of living, dynamic fellowships than to stay forever in a situation where they are constantly discouraged and, most likely, not being properly fed.

So, today, I can think of no circumstances in which one would be forbidden to leave a church or a denomination. If one makes such a change, for example, because he prefers the preaching in the new church, that may be a perfectly legitimate expression of need. Perhaps the first pastor's sermons were too simple or too difficult. We need to be where God's word addresses us meaningfully; otherwise we could worship in a language unknown to us! Perhaps one wishes to make a change because another church has a better Sunday school. To put it that way may seem to cater to the oft-despised "consumer mentality." But this may simply represent a desire to have better teaching for one's children; and that is a valid scriptural desire.

Some denominations erect unscriptural barriers against transfer, especially when it is a congregation rather than an individual that is seeking to make a move. Some denominations hold that they have a "proprietary interest" in their congregations, even to the point where the congregation's property is "held in trust for the denomination." The PCUSA has even taken congregations to secular courts (directly violating 1 Cor. 6:1–11) to maintain its supposed property rights. But no matter what the secular courts may say, the New Testament gives no such proprietary rights to any denomination. One might make a case to the effect that congregational property is held in trust for the *church;* but, as we have seen, "denomination" and "church" are not the same thing. So much confusion is caused by the inability to distinguish these two concepts!

Indeed, from an ecumenical point of view (to rejoin the main drift of this book), it would probably be best if there were more frequent transfers from one denomination to another, of both individuals and congregations. We need to tread down the denominational barriers over and over again. Perhaps then eventually they will fall so low that they won't ever be noticed again!

Notes

1. Remember Jeroboam: political division does not necessitate religious division.
2. Of course it is legitimate to honor the work that God did through the PCUS. But that can be done without "continuing" the denomination as such.

18

Short of Union, What?

I could wish that this book would sell millions of copies and touch off a mad stampede among Christians toward reunion of the one, true church. However, to be honest, I really don't have the faith to believe that this will happen. More likely, the book will stimulate some reflection, some discussion, and in time God might use it, together with many other providential factors, to lead his church toward some degree of deeper oneness. Full reunion could be a long way off, perhaps not until after Christ returns.[1]

Indeed, probably most readers of this book will not be in a position to wield significant influence to make major changes in the denominational configuration. Many of you are not pastors, bishops, elders, and the like. I am a minister, but that means only that I have one vote in my presbytery and one (sometimes) in General Assembly: one vote in a denomination (PCA) that is in my opinion rather uninterested in ecumenism, even suspicious of it.

So what short-term goals should we seek, by however small steps, as means toward the long-term goal of reunion? Let me make some suggestions:

Interdenominational Cooperation

If two denominations cannot merge, for one reason or another, certainly the next best thing is that they fellowship together as much as possible to get to know one another, break down stereotypes, persuade one another when that is necessary, and so on. Often, where conscience permits, this would include joint ministries of various kinds.

Among the tiny Presbyterian bodies where I spend most of my time, there is the concept of a "fraternal relationship." These relationships vary in detail, but usually the churches involved receive members from one another via letter of transfer, without requiring any additional examination or profession of faith. Ministerial transfer is somewhat more difficult, but usually at least without any stigma. Fraternal churches also exchange pulpits with a minimum of difficulty, and they send representatives to one another's presbytery and General Assembly meetings to bring greetings. Indeed, even ministers other than official representatives can be seated in the presbytery meetings of a fraternal denomination and be recognized (by vote) as "corresponding members" of the assembly, with privilege of the floor but not the right to vote.

The fraternal relationship is actually a kind of halfway union, for it presupposes that both denominations in the relationship accept the doctrinal and practical soundness of the other. Each body recognizes the soundness of the preaching, sacraments, and discipline of the other; each recognizes the wisdom and other gifts to be found in the other group.

Such fraternal relationships are an excellent way of becoming better acquainted, where that is thought to be necessary. My major problem with it is that in many cases they seem to be used as an illegitimate substitute for actual union. When two denominations recognize the soundness of one another's ministry, sacraments, and discipline to the extent of permitting such levels of joint ministry, one may rightly ask, why not go all the way to union? What can legitimately prevent union when two bodies so freely exchange members and preachers?

Indeed I have experienced the odd spectacle of sitting in a union discussion where fellow elders criticized a *fraternal church* as "not of like faith and practice." Although these elders wanted to maintain the fraternal relation, they did not want to merge. But if two churches are so different in faith and practice that they should not merge, then they should not be fraternal churches either. Surely, if two churches are fraternally related, the issue of whether they are alike in faith and practice is already settled. Union talks ought to focus on other matters.

Nevertheless, fraternal relations are better than no contact, and they can provide a kind of compromise when two denominations are considering union but want first to overcome their skittishness.

Another sort of preunion relationship might be an organization of denominations (most likely within the same confessional family) that covenant together to work toward union. An example is the National Association of Presbyterian and Reformed Churches (NAPARC), which meets regularly for interdenominational discussions and to share suggestions about ways of preunion cooperation. This is something similar to what I called earlier an "evangelical COCU." NAPARC has been a useful organization, and I recommend this approach to other confessional groupings.

Para-Church Ministries

Much of the work of the gospel today is carried out not through churches and denominations, but through organizations not officially connected with such bodies, known as para-church ministries. Examples would be Inter-Varsity Christian Fellowship, Campus Crusade For Christ, Young Life, the Billy Graham Evangelistic Association, independent mission boards like the Sudan Interior Mission, independent publications like *Christianity Today,* independent seminaries like Westminster Theological Seminary (where I teach), and publishers like Baker Book House without denominational connection.

Some people are very critical of such ministries, arguing that all the work of the church ought to be done by churches and denominations, not by independent groups.

I agree that only the church is appointed by God to carry out the Great Commission. Only the church has the mandate to do the work of the church. But what *is* the church? I have argued in this book that "the church" is the one, true church of the New Testament—a church that has been marred by denominationalism but has not been entirely destroyed. The highest court of the one, true church still exists and, indeed, is doing its job very well! I speak of the throne of Jesus at the right hand of God in heaven who rules his church as the head of the body. And the "lowest" courts of the one, true church also still exist and still function: the rulers of the local congregations. The problem is in the middle-level courts. To whom may a local congregation appeal when they have a problem too hard for them to resolve (as in Exod. 18:26)? God's plan was to have united rule of the church within larger regional units, but that rule has broken down. Replacing it has been denominational rule. So a local church in this position cannot appeal to a court of the *church* as a whole; it can appeal only to a *denominational* court, one that rules those within a particular *faction* of the church.

Christians recognize almost instinctively, I think, that there is something wrong here. God's intention is not to restrict us to using the wisdom and other gifts only from believers in our own denomination. His intention is that *all* Christians share their gifts with one another as members of Christ's body. Denominationalism naturally and unconsciously frustrates this purpose of mutual sharing. But, beyond this, do denominations have the right consciously to *prevent* such sharing from taking place? That is what happens when denominations demand that we work in ministry together only with people from our own denomination. Do they have such a right?

We need to recognize that in an important sense, *denominations themselves are para-church organizations*. God did not authorize denominations. As we have seen, they play no role in the government of the New Testament church. Denominations are the result of human sin. It is not wrong for us to use them, to approximate somewhat the sort of government ordained in Scripture. But they do not have the exclusive right to govern the ministry of God's people. Indeed, as I have argued, it is wrong for them to call themselves churches, as in "Church of the Brethren." Nothing like a denomination is ever called a church in the Bible.

Denominations are, to put it paradoxically, para-church organizations that we have set up to govern the church and to carry on much of its ministry. But there is no reason why, in the current fractured condition of the universal church, there should not be *other* para-church organizations, formed for purposes other than basic government and uniting Christians at other levels than those of denominations.

I can agree, again, that only the church is to carry out the Great Commission. But that is very different from saying that only *denominations* may carry out the Great Commission. That second point is the one being made by critics of para-church organizations, and I think it is quite wrong. Scripture does not give to denominations exclusive rights to govern Christian ministry.

Para-church ministries are the result of an intense hunger within the church to get together. We know in our hearts that we lack the resources within our individual congregations and denominations to do everything that needs to be done. We need to be able to benefit from *all* the gifts Jesus gives his body. Although we know that total reunion in the near future is not likely, humanly speaking, we rightly ask why we should not unite to meet some special needs that cannot easily be met by denominations working separately, like college ministry, city-wide evangelism, and so on.

Another argument against para-church ministries is that they are not subject to church discipline. But that is not necessarily true. Certainly the general rule is that leaders of para-church organizations are members of churches and of denominations and therefore subject to church discipline. Doubtless there is some awkwardness in the fact that the same organization may have leaders who are members of many different churches and denominations and that the total organization is not answerable to any church. But this is an awkwardness created by denominationalism itself; and that sort of awkwardness is certainly not a compelling argument against the concept.

Like fraternal relationships, but in a different way, para-church ministries are a kind of halfway house to union. They allow us to share gifts, as Scripture provides and requires, without actual organizational union. They provide opportunities to fellowship and minister together, opportunities that, for many, are prerequisites to union.

All in all, I encourage the development of para-church ministries. I see nothing against them in Scripture, and experience shows that God has made good use of them, for the most part. We should not, however, be satisfied with them alone. We should work toward the day in which a reunited church will take back upon itself all its ministry responsibilities.

And of course a warning is in order to those Christians who avoid the churches and seek to get all their Christian fellowship and edification in para-church organizations. That, too, is not God's way. To paraphrase a Christian cartoon I recall from some years ago, Jesus founded a church, not a Christian coffee house. He wants his people to be under the oversight and teaching of ordained elders and to receive the sacraments.

Partial Unions

We need to think more creatively about possible steps to reunion. There are various ways short of total union that denominations can move in the direction of reunion.

Consider a union discussion between a presbyterian body that sings only musical arrangements of Old Testament Psalms (such as the Reformed Presbyterian Church of North America) and a body that rejects that restriction (such as the Orthodox Presbyterian Church).

Let us say that tolerance is not an option in this case, that the RPCNA representatives demand that their convictions be maintained in their churches with the force of discipline.

In this case one solution might be to allow congregations to discipline according to their convictions on this matter, but that persons so disciplined by a local congregation would not have the option of appealing to a higher court. Another possibility, more favorable to the RPCNA position, might be to group the former RPCNA congregations into "Psalm-singing presbyteries," which would use their discipline to require exclusive Psalm singing in their congregations. These presbyteries would be linked to the former OPC presbyteries in a General Assembly governing both; but discipline cases over Psalm singing could not be appealed to General Assembly, but would have to be resolved at the presbytery level.

That is not really a complete church union, but it is a union for most practical purposes. Similarly, episcopal churches could set aside certain dioceses for the enforcement of minority positions that cannot otherwise be honored. Congregational churches, of course, would not have this sort of problem, since therein each congregation is relatively autonomous in any case, and since appeals, when possible, are handled only by *ad hoc* assemblies.

Voluntary Realignment

In the late 1960s, when renewed discussion began of merger between the northern (PCUSA) and southern (PCUS) Presbyterian churches, some people (mostly conservatives) proposed that instead of merger, the churches be open to "voluntary realignment." What that meant was that ministers, members, and congregations would be free to join whichever of the two denominations they pleased. These people expected that liberals would leave the southern church to join the northern church, and conservatives vice versa, leaving the southern church more conservative and the northern church more liberal, but allowing both to function as nationwide bodies. That idea was never approved or implemented.

More recently, as I have mentioned, several congregations of the OPC have left to join the PCA, seeking to "realign" with others with more similar priorities. I was among them. Comments:

1. In some ways, realignment is counterproductive to eventual reunion. For it leaves denominations more different from one another

than before. It also often stirs up resentments within the denomination from which a group departs.

2. Normally, realignment is not desirable when it is merely a means of finding a denomination more in agreement with one's own priorities. In general, it is better to have different kinds of priorities represented in each denomination. Homemakers and breadwinners should be together. (Recall chapter 12.)

3. However, these considerations must be balanced against the overriding importance of the Great Commission. If the priorities of a denomination keep someone from carrying out the ministry to which God has called him, then he ought to realign.

4. In general, it is best that realignment be made easy, as I argued in the last chapter. This is not only permitted by Scripture, but it is also important to the prospect of reunion. I do believe that Christians instinctively want to "get together." When they are allowed to move easily from one denomination to another, they will tend to form large groups in which the diversity of the Spirit's gifts is maximized. That is helpful to the prospect of reunion.

Intradenominational Policies

There are many denominational policies that need to be rethought in view of the points I have been making; for many of these policies are detrimental to the prospects for reunion and have nothing to recommend them except denominational chauvinism. I mentioned some of these in the last chapter—for example, the policy of some churches to insist that the denomination has a "proprietary interest" in its congregations. Another example: The Christian Reformed Church requires that all its candidates for the ministry attend its own seminary, Calvin Theological Seminary, for at least one year, even if they have a seminary degree from another institution, and that they be recommended to the church by the seminary faculty as a prerequisite to ordination.[2] Calvin has among the most difficult entrance requirements of any seminary. These requirements make it very difficult for anyone not of Christian Reformed Church background to enter the ministry of the church. Doubtless this requirement was formulated at a time when the heavily ethnic Dutch church, wary of American cultural influences, desired to safeguard its future orthodoxy. Ironically, it has now happened that Calvin Seminary itself has come under fire by some in the denomination.

I will not here try to determine who is most correct in the controversy between Calvin Seminary's supporters and detractors. I think that
the very fact that suspicions exist is a problem, because it shows there is
lack of trust within the body. That lack of trust, I believe, is itself
related to the denomination's seminary policy. On that policy, not on
the theology of the Calvin faculty, I do intend to express an opinion.

There is, for one thing, no way to keep "outside influences" out of
a denomination or a seminary. Seminary professors, even those born
and raised within a denomination, usually at some point go outside
the denomination for advanced training. That training is often considered a necessity, for theological professors are supposed to be aware of
the latest scholarship. They often receive this training at the hands of
scholars with theological views that would not be acceptable in a conservative denomination. We like to hope that such advanced students
have the discernment to judge rightly what in their instruction is com-
patible with orthodoxy and what is not, but such hopes are not always
fulfilled. Where students have not been discerning, the church must be
vigilant to exercise its proper discipline. But one thing is clear:
Certainly those who accept such opportunities for training are going
to bring back with them "outside influences," for better or worse.
Otherwise, what is the point of the training?

For other reasons, too, it is impossible to keep "outside ideas" from
influencing a denomination. In the modern world, information is
spread rapidly and widely and by many media. More seriously, God
himself opposes the insulation of denominations from others; for his
true church is not limited to one denomination, and he wants his sons
and daughters to communicate freely to one another their love and
their knowledge. Indeed, the best protection for denominational
orthodoxy is not to bar the doors against invasion from outside, but
rather to be open to what God is teaching the *whole* body of Christ
through the Scriptures. To facilitate this process, denominations need
new blood from time to time; or, to change the metaphor, they need
to be cross-fertilized by other segments of the body. Left entirely to
itself, no denomination has sufficient resources to guard its orthodoxy
or vitality. From this isolation come problems of unorthodoxy or of
unjustified *suspicion* of unorthodoxy—lack of trust.

Evangelical denominations that try to bar the door against the
influence of evangelicals of other backgrounds—but that welcome college and seminary professors with training in institutions (usually liberal or outrightly non-Christian) outside the denomination—have the
worst of all possible worlds. They open themselves on the one hand to

the possibility or suspicion of liberal influence, but on the other hand they deny to themselves the help of God's gifts to the body outside their own circles.

Let us seek to break down any structures in our denominations that serve only to discourage outsiders from joining us. A denomination has the right to examine ministerial candidates, to guard the orthodoxy of its ministry. But it should not keep people out of its ministry only because they have a different background, have not mastered denominational buzz-words, and/or have different priorities from the majority of the denomination.

Toward a Trans-Denominational Loyalty

Finally, I urge that we discourage the tendency in our communions toward denominational chauvinism: that is, wasting God's time promoting the interests of our denomination over against those of others.

In the events noted earlier, when several congregations moved from OPC to PCA, a lot of tears were shed. Tears are appropriate at any parting; see Acts 20:36–38. But these tears were not simply mourning the loss of close contact. Rather, they often had a different meaning.

One man wept because some of his family had been part of one of these congregations for many years and had made many contributions to it; now their church was being taken away from them. Now they would have no place to go to church! I tried to sympathize with my brother, but I confess to some feeling of outrage. No place to go to church? It was not as if the church was going defunct or merging with a liberal congregation. It was only changing from one evangelical Presbyterian denomination to another! Surely the past contributions of this family were not going to be lost or negated; rather they were going to be fulfilled in a new phase of the church's ministry. The tears, I fear, were tears of denominational chauvinism—tears for which the Scriptures show no sympathy.

Another man wept because he and his church had supplied money and leadership to one of the churches that were leaving. Now, said the elder, that church is "gone." Gone? Only gone to another denomination!

Still another man, noting that two of those advocating the transfers taught at Westminster Seminary in California,[3] proposed that the OPC establish its own seminary, so that OPC ministerial candidates might not have to sit under the baleful influence of "realigners." This elder wanted a seminary that would almost uncritically support the OPC, recommending the OPC to its students, above all other denominations, as a place of service. In my view, that, too, is denominational chauvinism. A faculty member would have to be intellectually dishonest to present the OPC as the only legitimate home for evangelical Presbyterians; for in fact there are several other denominations that sincerely subscribe to precisely the same doctrines as the OPC and that display the other marks of the true church discussed earlier.

My prize for denominational chauvinism[4] goes to the OPC General Assembly several years ago that determined that no home missions aid be given to any congregation failing to use "Orthodox Presbyterian Church" in its church name. Many of our churches had not used that name, because it was not well understood in their communities and was "turning off" visitors. That particular General Assembly evidently put a higher value on denominational publicity than on reaching communities with the gospel.

It is right to promote what God is doing in your own denomination and to seek to attract workers and new members there. It is wrong to promote your denomination at the expense of others who have a common faith and practice.

Much more could be said on this subject, but I trust the reader has the main idea by now. Let us think of ourselves more and more as members of the body of Christ, and less and less as denominational partisans. When we make plans, let us ask ourselves seriously how these plans will help or hinder the unity of the church. And somehow, let's get together.

Notes

1. On the other hand: God keeps rebuking my lack of faith. If communism in Europe can collapse over a year's time, why not denominationalism?

2. In addition to my other problems with this arrangement, which shall be evident shortly, I question strongly the scriptural basis for giving to a seminary faculty virtual veto power over ordinations.

3. Several other Westminster faculty members, however, were strongly opposed.

4. Close runner-up: the elder who insisted that "not one penny" of the money given to his denomination should ever go to the support of anyone in another denomination.

19

• •

What Do We Do Now?

I have said that I am not the practical sort of person who can set forth an efficient program for achieving the unity I have advocated. At this point, I feel with a peculiar intensity the need for gifts that God has given to other believers than myself! However, I have made a few specific suggestions that may deserve consideration, and I have a few more to share. Let me close this volume by assembling from the body of this book various concrete suggestions that should advance the cause of reunion, adding here and there a few others that occur to me.

1. Cultivate new ways of thinking (both theoretically and practically) about the church, which avoid the temptation to confuse "church" with "denomination" (chapter 3).

2. Avoid thinking of your denomination as a kind of home team ("denominational chauvinism"), which you will always support against the others no matter how untenable its positions and actions (chapter 5).

3. Pray that God will speed his own reunion plan to completion (chapter 6).

4. Get involved in situations such as neighborhood Bible studies and chaplaincies where you are forced to share fellowship and/or ministry

with Christians from other traditions. Allow the sense of unity you gain from such experiences to color your view of the church (chapter 7).

5. Recognize that doctrinal toleration is unavoidable, and therefore ask seriously to what extent it might be extended (or reduced!) in our denominations, to draw each denomination closer to Christians outside it (chapter 8). For example, the Evangelical Free Church might well consider whether it is really helpful to require professors at Trinity Evangelical Divinity School to subscribe to premillennialism. Are they really so sure of that teaching that they can justify insulating the denomination from alternative views, especially when they allow tolerance concerning matters such as predestination and the subjects of baptism? (And what good are they doing themselves and their theology students by preventing them from studying with godly scholars who hold other views?) But always seek to distinguish a proper tolerance from theological indifference.

6. Look at other denominations that disagree doctrinally with your own in a somewhat different way: not as people who have rejected God's truth,[1] but as people who have not been taught by God as we have, who perhaps have not had a fair opportunity even to consider (in an unbiased atmosphere) the teachings we cherish (chapter 8).

7. Engage in doctrinal discussion less polemically, seeking to do justice to the legitimate concerns of the other side, remembering that the great gulf is not between believers of different convictions, but between believers and unbelievers (chapter 8).

8. Be open to what God has been teaching other denominations (chapter 8).

9. Ask God for the right combination of commitment and teachability. Be willing then to admit that some of what your denomination believes might be wrong and that God may have given insight to some other branch of the church (chapter 8).

10. Seek involvement of other denominations when there are doctrinal disputes in your own. Seek to turn doctrinal debates into occasions for the whole church, or as much of it as possible, to study together (chapter 8).

11. Consider some degree of increased toleration by explicit agreement, as a means of union between church bodies. The Evangelical Presbyterian Church has declared itself open to various views considering women elders and charismatic gifts. In my view, the EPC is actually *too* tolerant in these particular areas, but I do see other areas in which this strategy might be wisely implemented. For example, the

Orthodox Presbyterian Church and the Reformed Presbyterian Church of North America are largely agreed on everything except that the latter denomination uses Psalm versions exclusively in worship. Certainly these bodies ought to merge, explicitly allowing each congregation to make its own decision in this matter, or perhaps even providing for some exclusive Psalm-singing presbyteries (chapter 8).

12. For now, refrain from writing new creeds. I say that most reluctantly, for there is a need for new affirmations and denials by the churches, addressed to contemporary situations. A truly ecumenical creed, one to which Christians of all denominations would subscribe, would be an excellent development. (I do applaud recent creeds by para-church groups like the International Council for Biblical Inerrancy and the Council For Biblical Manhood and Womanhood.) Unfortunately, however, most contemporary creeds are limited to one denomination, and no denomination has the right to speak for the one, true church. Further, once a denomination adopts a new creed, the new creed separates it more sharply from other denominations that have not adopted it. Union with other denominations is therefore made more difficult.

13. Escalate the fight against theological liberalism. There will be no union worthy of the name unless it excludes those who will not place themselves under the supreme authority of God's word. The process of isolating and excluding liberal teaching from our churches is one that may, and ought to, begin now. Twenty-five years ago, it was widely taught that once a denomination had become infected with liberal teaching it could not be brought back to the truth. Since that time, however, evangelical movements in several denominations infected with liberalism have made good strides toward biblical reformation: the Lutheran Church—Missouri Synod, the Southern Baptist Convention, and the Associate Reformed Presbyterian Church are some examples. It can be done! And once the confusing influence of liberalism is removed, we will see much more clearly to deal with those real doctrinal differences that remain. There is no room for unbelief in the one, true church of Jesus Christ.

14. In general, respect the discipline of other churches and denominations. When someone seeks to join your church to escape discipline somewhere else, do not simply welcome that person in with no questions asked. Do some investigating. It may be the judgment of your church that the discipline of another church was unfair or unnecessarily harsh, and it is not wrong to disagree with another body in the

absence of a higher court to resolve the matter decisively. But never let your zeal for grabbing a new member interfere with your responsibility to the whole church of Jesus Christ.

15. Read what others say about your denomination and/or theological tradition—and not just to refute them.

16. Consider revising the subscription vows taken by officers in your church/denomination to encourage the balance between doctrinal unity and healthy doctrinal change discussed in chapter 8.

17. Mute polemics as much as conscience permits.

18. Do not insist on rebaptizing or reordaining people who enter your denomination from another orthodox (Nicene Creed) body (chapter 9). When someone claims that he has been baptized or ordained, take his word for it, unless you have strong evidence to the contrary.

19. Find three good jokes about your own denomination or tradition and share them with your fellow members.

20. Practice open communion (chapter 9).

21. Develop a form of worship that welcomes believers from other traditions (chapter 9).

22. Forgive personal and corporate injuries done to you by those of other bodies (chapter 10).

23. Don't worry so much about details of church government; worry more about the spiritual qualities of those who govern (chapter 11).

24. Follow the servant model whenever you are in a position of authority (chapter 11).

25. Be more self-critical of your own and your denomination's priorities (chapter 12).

26. Consider the possibility that the differences between your denomination and others may be to some extent differences in priority or emphasis rather than substantive differences (chapter 12).

27. Maintain a biblical balance of emphasis in your church's preaching and teaching ministry, avoiding overemphasis of denominational distinctives.

28. Examine yourself and your denomination to purge the attitudes listed in chapter 13.

29. Examine yourself and your denomination to purge the assumptions discussed in chapter 14.

30. Seek to convert your church's emphasis and mentality to an "outward facing" one, working to eliminate "ingrownness" (chapter 15).

31. Insist that critics of other denominations bear the burden of proof under strict standards of evidence; regard those denominations as innocent until proven guilty (chapter 16). Do not settle for gossip, no matter how much that gossip reinforces your denominational self-image.

32. Allow relatively free and easy transfer between your denomination and others, at least within your own tradition (chapters 17, 18).

33. Loosen unreasonable restrictions designed to make it difficult for people outside your denomination to enter the ministry of your denomination (chapter 18).

34. Where organizational union is not a practical goal, seek the sorts of pre-union relationships described in chapter 18.

Notes

1. All of us do, of course, sometimes reject God's truth, and denominations sometimes do that corporately. My point is that this is not the only reason for doctrinal disagreement, and it is wise for us to consider other reasons as well.

Appendix
Peacemakers
Dennis E. Johnson

My colleague Dennis Johnson preached this message at our daily morning devotional service at Westminster Seminary in California. His original audience was composed mostly of people studying for the ministry, but the basic thrust applies to all of us. I feel that it provides a good positive counterpart to chapter 13 of this book and an challenging note on which to end. If you seriously apply yourself to being a peacemaker in the biblical sense, you will accomplish, consciously or not, all the goals enumerated in this volume. Copies of the address can be obtained from the seminary at 1725 Bear Valley Parkway, Escondido, CA 92027, or phone (619) 480-8474. My thanks to the seminary and to Dennis for their permission to use it here.

Peacemakers
Matthew 5:9

Dennis E. Johnson, Ph. D.
Associate Professor of New Testament
Westminster Theological Seminary in California

"Blessed are the peacemakers, for they will be called sons of God."
Christ calls you to a complicated, painful, and blessed task: *making peace.* It is not a task at which leaders in Reformed or Evangelical churches are especially good. I suspect that it is not a top priority in

170

prospective students' choice of a seminary: "I want to become a peace-maker, so I'm going to Westminster." For many of us the picture that stirs our imagination is that of Christian soldiers marching into war against the forces of atheism, liberalism, pragmatism, and sometimes anything and anyone that is less that 99 44/100% pure presupposi-tional, biblical-theological, nouthetic Calvinism.[1] The denominations in which we serve were born out of the trauma of doctrinal conflict over the central truths of God's Word. Those conflicts were necessary and right. So we know that it's right to contend valiantly for the truth; but we're not so sure about whether it's OK to get along with Christians who don't see the truth exactly as we do.

1. A Complicated Task

To be a *biblical* peacemaker, you need to develop a bias toward com-promise on unimportant points, rather than insisting on confrontation at every point of disagreement. Be willing to place a priority on the common ground which Christians share, rather than focusing exclu-sively on our differences. Be willing to place the best interpretation on the motives and actions of others, rather than approaching them suspi-ciously, assuming the worst about their hidden agendas. You need a lot of patient trust in God, that he will show them where they are wrong—and you where you are wrong!

But here is what makes this job so complicated: Which *are* the unim-portant points of difference on which you can compromise for the pres-ent? What if the pragmatic methods that your brother uses in evange-lism really *are* rooted in a man-centered gospel, or motivated by a thirst for power and fame rather than compassion for sinful people and a pas-sion for the glory of God? God's peace does not peacefully coexist with falsehood, sham, or injustice; so God's peacemakers cannot simply ignore peace-destroying sin and error, any more than a surgeon can simply close up an infected wound: an abscess is bound to develop.

And yet, on the other hand, "love *does* cover over a multitude of sins" (1 Peter 4:8). What sins or differences of conviction can be covered? Which ones must be confronted in humble love for your brother or sis-ter? It's a complicated task, and because of that it is also. . . .

2. A Painful Task

Making peace is not easy. To be a peacemaker you have to become the person that all the other Beatitudes describe. Peacemaking demands that you be *poor in spirit,* humble enough to admit that you have been wrong and to ask for forgiveness (as Jesus commands later in this ser-mon, Matt. 5:23–24). It demands *meekness,* which shows itself in the self-control to hold your tongue, to refuse to use the truth sometimes, even though it would vindicate your cause and blow your opponent out of the water (Matt. 5:22). It demands that the stains and the schisms in the church, the body of Christ, bother you—a lot!—so that you *mourn* as you survey the ravages of sin in yourself and your brothers and sisters.

And sometimes peacemaking is painful because the Christians among whom you are trying to make peace will disagree with you on whether compromise or confrontation is the way to peace in a particular situation. They may just think you have poor judgment—naively optimistic, theologically undiscerning, etc.: "If you *really* understood the underlying theological issues, the actual motivations of our opponents, you would know that peace will never come through negotiation or compromise, but only through those opponents' unconditional surrender." Or they may suspect *your* motives, too: "Why aren't you willing to pay the price to contend for the faith once-for-all delivered to the saints?" Peacemakers can look like cowardly "pleasers of men" when they are compared with bold champions who courageously disregard the opinions and feelings of human beings.

My hunch is that Barnabas was more characteristically a peacemaker than was Paul: Could this be the source of their friction over taking John Mark along on a second trip (Acts 15:36–41)? Barnabas wanted to give Mark a second chance. But from Paul's perspective, perhaps, Barnabas looked naive when he hoped that Mark had learned his lesson from his first desertion. So they disagreed—sharply! They argued. And biblical peace was fractured. Now, I've heard this passage appealed to to justify denominationalism, but I think you have to say that the Holy Spirit was *not* smiling in approval as he caused Luke to report this scene. *Somebody* was in the wrong. Maybe Paul was right and Barnabas was wrong: Mark wasn't ready yet. Maybe Barnabas was right: later Paul did appreciate Mark's ministry (2 Tim. 4:11). In any case, Barnabas the peacemaker *looked* wrong to Paul, and neither man would budge.

If you set out to be a peacemaker in Christ's church, you will not always make the right choice about how to preserve the unity of the Spirit in the bond of peace. And even when you do make the right choice, it's going to look wrong to lots of people: to some, too tolerant; to others, too rigid. You can't win. . . . Oh, yes, you can:

3. A Blessed Task

The task is blessed because Jesus says so, and he announces the amazing honor which will be bestowed on peacemakers at the last judgment: "they will be called sons of God." Or, to make plain the real subject who stands behind this divine passive: "God will call them his sons."

In one way or another, all of the promises of the Beatitudes are promises of eternal life and joy in the kingdom of God; but each promise focuses on a particular aspect of that complete salvation. What is the special focus of being called by God as his sons?

a. As sons peacemakers are *in tune with the Father's purpose*. God's goal is peace, not conflict. Unity, not division and hostility. The pastor of the congregation in which I worship was preaching on James's description of heavenly wisdom this past Sunday: "Peacemakers who sow in peace raise a harvest of righteousness" (3:18). He observed that righteousness does not grow in an environment of strife, competition, and hostility. Farming may not be as exciting as the battlefield, but the patient planting and watering of reconciliation, patience, and forgiveness produces the fruit of righteous lives and attitudes which delight our Father. Make it your goal to *win over* those who differ from you rather than simply to *win* over them, and you will show that you are pursuing the purpose of the Father.

b. As sons, peacemakers *reflect the image of God's Son*. If you think that peacemaking is painful for you, look at Jesus. If you are hurting from the criticism which you have had to absorb in your efforts to promote peace in Christ's church, consider the price he paid for our peace. Christ's purpose "was to create in himself one new man out of the two, thus *making peace*, and in this one body to reconcile both of them to God *through the cross*, by which he put to death their hostility" (Eph. 2:15–16). Peacemakers are blessed, despite the pain and the criticism, because in them is reflected the peacemaking grace of the Son of God, who gave himself to reconcile us to God and to each other.

I have a dream. Actually, I have a lot of dreams for Westminster in California, as many of us do. But here is one of mine: That when public awareness surveys about seminaries are taken in future years, knowledgeable Christians will say about Westminster in California: "That school is committed to the lordship of Christ, the authority of Scripture, the Reformed faith, and high standards of scholarship; *and that school is committed to producing peacemakers*. That seminary is committed to a loving, patient, gentle, even *tolerant* pursuit of peace with all kinds of Christians, even those who are not as committed as Westminster is to Christ's lordship, the Bible, Reformed theology, and scholarship." My hope is that the day will come when, if a church is facing trauma and turmoil and is in need of healing, its leaders will say, "We need a Westminster in California graduate to lead us by his example and his teaching so that we will learn to preserve the unity of the Spirit in the bond of peace."

It is complicated and painful, but it is also a blessed task to be peace-makers, showing the gracious patience of the Son of God, who has made us God's sons. And it is *your* task as a disciple of Jesus the Son, the Peacemaker.

Notes

1. "Presuppositionalism," "biblical-theological method," "nouthetic counseling" and "militant Calvinism" are known to be distinctive emphases of Westminster Seminary in California.

Bibliography

Alder, Susan. "Background: An Interview with R. J. Rushdoony on Church Government." *Christian Observer,* 3 November 1989, pp. 17-18.

Arn, Win. "America—the Mission Field," *The Win Arn Growth Report.* Pasadena, Calif.: 1986, pp. 3–4.

Bannerman, James. *The Church of Christ.* London: Banner of Truth, 1960.

Berkouwer, G. C. *The Church.* Grand Rapids: Eerdmans, 1976.

Clowney, Edmund P. *The Doctrine of the Church.* Philadelphia: Presbyterian and Reformed, 1976.

Frame, J. *Doctrine of the Knowledge of God.* Phillipsburg, N.J.: Presbyterian and Reformed, 1987.

Jordan, J. "One in the Spirit," in *Presbyterian Heritage* 10 (Sept. 1986): 1–4.

———. ed. *The Reconstruction of the Church,* Christianity and Civilization 4. Tyler, Tex.: Geneva Ministries, 1985.

———. *The Sociology of the Church.* Tyler, Tex.: Geneva Ministries, 1986.

———. *Through New Eyes.* Brentwood, Tenn.: Wolgemuth and Hyatt, 1988.

Kuhn, Thomas. *The Structure of Scientific Revolutions.* Chicago: Univ. of Chicago Press, 1962, 1970.

Kuiper, R. B. *The Glorious Body of Christ.* London: Banner of Truth, 1967.

Machen, J. Gresham. *Christianity and Liberalism.* Grand Rapids: Eerdmans, 1923.

MacLeod, Donald. "Ecumenism: Lessons From Vancouver '89." *Outlook,* December 1989, pp. 15-18.

M'Crie, Thomas. *The Unity of the Church.* Dallas: Presbyterian Heritage Publications, 1989; originally Edinburgh: W. Blackwood, 1821.

Miller, C. John. *Outgrowing the Ingrown Church.* Grand Rapids: Ministry Resources Library, 1986.

Murray, John. "The Biblical Basis for Ecclesiastical Union." In *Collected Writings, I.* Edinburgh: Banner of Truth, 1976, pp. 269–272.

———. *Christian Baptism,* Philadelphia: Presbyterian and Reformed, 1952.

———. "Corporate Responsibility." *Collected Writings, I.* Edinburgh: Banner of Trust, 1976, pp. 273–279.

———. "The Creedal Basis of Union in the Church." Ibid., pp. 273-279.

———. *Divorce.* Grand Rapids: Baker, 1961.

———. "Government in the Church of Christ." *Collected Writings I.* Edinburgh: Banner of Truth, 1976, pp. 260–268, pp. 260–268.

Poythress, Vern. *Symphonic Theology.* Grand Rapids: Zondervan, 1987.

———. *Understanding Dispensationalists.* Grand Rapids: Zondervan, 1988.

Reed, Kevin. *Biblical Church Government.* Dallas: Presbyterian Heritage, 1983.

Van Til, Cornelius. *Christianity and Barthianism.* Grand Rapids: Baker, 1962.

———. *The Defense of the Faith.* Phillipsburg, N.J.: Presbyterian and Reformed, 1975.

Wright, D., and Ferguson, Sinclair, ed. *New Dictionary of Theology.* Leicester, England: Inter-Varsity Press, 1988.

Subject Index

177

Scripture Index

181

2